High-Protein Vegan Cookbook

Healthy & Delicious Plant Based Recipes

Charlotte Melhoff

© Copyright 2018 by Charlotte Melhoff - All rights reserved.

Transmission, duplication or reproduction of any of the following work including specific information will be considered an illegal act irrespective of if it is done electronically or in print. This extends to creating a secondary or tertiary copy of the work or a recorded copy and is only allowed with express written consent from the Publisher. All additional right reserved.

The information in the following pages is broadly considered to be a truthful and accurate account of facts and as such any inattention, use or misuse of the information in question by the reader will render any resulting actions solely under their purview. There are no scenarios in which the publisher or the original author of this work can be in any fashion deemed liable for any hardship or damages that may befall them after undertaking information described herein.

Additionally, the information in the following pages is intended only for informational purposes and should thus be thought of as universal. As befitting its nature, it is presented without assurance regarding its prolonged validity or interim quality. Trademarks that are mentioned are done without written consent and can in no way be considered an endorsement from the trademark holder.

Table of Contents

Introduction 7
Chapter One: Basics of a High-Protein Vegan Diet 9
   Different Types of Vegan 9
- ☐ Junk-Food Vegan Diet 9
- ☐ The Thrive Diet 10
- ☐ Raw-till-4 10
- ☐ The Starch Solution 10
- ☐ 80/10/10 10
- ☐ Whole-Food Vegan Diet 10

   What to Eat 11
      Vegetables and Fruits 11
      Seeds, Nuts, and Legumes 12
      Whole Grains 12
      Vegan Food Products and Substitutions 13

   Foods to Avoid 13
      Poultry, Meat, and Seafood 13
      Dairy and Eggs 13
      Animal-Based Ingredients 14

   Best Protein Sources 14
1. Fruits and Vegetables 14
2. Seeds, Nuts, and Nut Butters 15
3. Chia Seeds 15
4. Wild Rice 16
5. Oatmeal and Oats 16
6. Soy Milk 17
7. Sprouted Grains and Ezekiel Bread 17
8. Quinoa and Amaranth 17
9. Spirulina 18
10. Green Peas 18
11. Hempseed 19
12. Teff and Spelt 19
13. Nutritional Yeast 20
14. Chickpeas and Beans 20
15. Lentils 20
16. Edamame, Tempeh, and Tofu 21

17. Seitan 21
Primary Protein Functions.. 22
   1. Antibodies.. 22
   2. Storage and Transportation of Molecules 23
   3. Enzymes... 23
   4. Hormones.. 23
   5. Energy... 23
   6. Maintenance and Repair 24
   7. Muscular Health... 24
   8. Improved Bone Health................................... 24
How Much Protein?.. 25
Protein Deficiency 25
Side Effects from Protein 25
   1. Weight Gain 26
   2. Cardiovascular Issues..................................... 26
   3. Bone Health... 26
   4. Ammonia 26

Chapter Two: Breakfast Recipes 28
Leek, Mushroom, and Spinach Breakfast Scramble 29
Southwest Breakfast Tacos.. 31
Black Bean and Sweet Potato Breakfast Burrito 33
Tofu Scramble Burrito Bowl 36
Chickpea Breakfast Enchiladas...................................... 38
Quinoa with Tempeh 41
Coconut Split Pea Breakfast Porridge Bowl 43
Chickpea Pancakes 45
Falafel Waffles 48
Chia Zucchini Breakfast Muffins 50
Peanut Butter Protein Granola Bars 52
Overnight Oats... 54
Spicy Breakfast Skillet 56
Vegan Omelet 59
Country Hash... 62

Chapter Three: Lunch Recipes 65
Vegan Veggie Protein Burgers 65
Vegan High-Protein Chili 68
Vegan Mexican Quinoa 70
Protein Pasta Fagioli 72
Spicy Lentil Stew 74
Cauliflower and White Bean Alfredo Pasta 76
Quinoa Salad 79
Green Curry Tofu 81
African Peanut Protein Stew 84
Thai Zucchini Noodle Salad 86
Spicy Chickpea Sandwich 87
Split Pea and Cauliflower Stew 89
Black Bean and Pumpkin Chili 92
Matcha Tofu Soup 94
Sweet Potato Tomato Soup 96
Baked Spicy Tofu Sandwich 98
Vegetable Stir-Fry 101
Kale Protein Bowl 103

Chapter Four: Dinner Recipes 105
Veggie Pad Thai 105
Vegan Cheesy Mac and Cheese 108
Sweet Potato Gnocchi 110
Taco Pasta Bowl 112
Avocado Pasta 114
Broccoli Over Orzo 116
Garlic Zucchini and Lentils 118
Vegetable Shepherd's Pie 120
Vegan BBQ Tofu 123
Spicy Kung Pao Tofu 125
Easy Vegan Tacos 127
Lentil Burgers 129
Black Bean Meatloaf 131
Easy Noodle Alfredo 133
Hot Potato Curry 135
Spinach and Red Lentil Masala 137
Sweet Hawaiian Burger 139

Chapter Five: Snacks and Desserts..................................142
    Spicy Kale Chips 142
    Cinnamon and Maple Quinoa Granola............................. 144
    Five-Ingredient Protein Bars 146
    Peanut Butter Power Bites 148
    Black Bean Dip 150
    Chocolate Chip Protein Cookies.. 151
    Vegan Bean Brownies..153
    Delicious Dessert Pizza..155
    Vanilla and Almond Popsicles 158
    Oatmeal and Peanut Butter Cookies 159
    Passion Fruit Mousse 161
    Tiny Strawberry Shortcakes... 163

Chapter Six: Beverage Recipes 165
    Blueberry Breakfast Smoothie 165
    Chocolate Protein Smoothie..167
    Banana Protein Smoothie 168
    Peanut Butter, Chocolate, and Coconut Smoothie........... 169
    Vanilla Chai Smoothie 170
    "It's a Date" Smoothie 171
    Beet and Fig Smoothie 172
    Matcha and Kiwi Smoothie 173
    Green Cleansing Smoothie 175

Conclusion.. 176

Introduction

First off, I would like to congratulate you on making the decision to eat the Vegan way! You will be amazed by the benefits that eating whole foods can bring you. Within weeks, you may notice that you have more energy and feel greater than ever. On top of the added benefit of health, you will also be helping the environment and the animals. As you will soon be learning in the following chapters, fruits and vegetables do not need to be bland! You will be provided with dozens of delicious recipes for breakfast, lunch, and dinner.

Whether you are seasoned in the kitchen or a true beginner, *High-Protein Vegan Cookbook* was created for any individual who wishes to add vegan meals into their diet so that they can experience the incredible health results. All recipes that you find within this book are plant-based meals, which were created to celebrate the natural and rich flavors of your fruits and vegetables. You will find that the foods provide the nutritional value you need, which can help you fight disease and lose weight.

If you are exploring veganism for the first time, I invite you to spend some quality time within the first chapter of this book. Together, we will go over the basics of the vegan diet so that you may have a clear understanding of the rules that entail the diet and why getting a proper amount of protein is so important. With this information, you will also be learning what you can and cannot eat if you wish to become vegan.

Once you have a clear understanding of a Vegan diet, you will be learning all about high-protein foods that you will be consuming. There are many myths behind the vegan diet such as lack of nutrients and vitamins now that you will no longer be consuming animal products. The truth is, nature provides us with *everything* we need! When you feel confident with the rules of the diet, then it is time to get to the fun action: cooking!

I hope that by the end of this book, you will be inspired to create the flavorful and protein-packed meals provided within this chapter. Each recipe is quick, easy-to-follow, and packed with the vitamins and nutrients that you need to maintain a healthy balance through breakfast, lunch, and dinner. I have assured to include a wide variety of recipes to appease even the skeptical carnivore in your life. Enjoy!

Chapter One: Basics of a High-Protein Vegan Diet

There are a million and one diets on the market currently. If you can dream of it, the diet probably already exists. The vegan diet is one that has been growing in popularity for a number of reasons. While some turn to veganism for ethical reasons, others consider the vegan diet for environmental purposes and even health reasons. When this diet is followed correctly, there are some wonderful health benefits that happen when you begin eating healthy. Before I get ahead of myself, let's learn what the Vegan diet is in the first place!

Different Types of Vegan

To put it in layman's terms, Veganism is about adopting a lifestyle that excludes any form of animal cruelty or exploitation. This includes any purpose, whether it be for clothing or for food. For these reasons, the Vegan diet gets rid of any animal products such as dairy, eggs, and meat. With that being said, there are several different types of vegan diets. These include:

- **Junk-Food Vegan Diet**

    A Junk-Food Vegan diet consists of mock meats, vegan desserts, fries, cheese, and heavily processed vegan foods. As you will learn later in this book, our diet avoids these foods. While technically, they are "vegan," this doesn't mean that they are good for you.

- **The Thrive Diet**

    This version of the Vegan diet is based around raw foods. The individuals who choose to follow this diet eat only whole foods that are either raw or, at the very least, cooked at very low temperatures.

- **Raw-till-4**

    The Raw-till-4 diet is just as it sounds. This diet is low-fat, where raw foods are consumed until about four at night. After four, individuals can have a fully-cooked plant-based meal for their dinner.

- **The Starch Solution**

    This version is very close to the 80/10/10 diet, which you will be learning about next. The starch solution diet follows a diet that is low-fat and high-carb. This type of vegan will focus on foods such as corn, rice, and potatoes instead of fruits.

- **80/10/10**

    This diet is another version of the Raw-Food Vegan diet. Vegans who undergo this try to limit their fat intake from foods such as avocados and nuts. It is most commonly known as the fruitarian diet or the raw-food vegan diet because individuals focus on soft greens and raw fruits while following this diet.

- **Whole-Food Vegan Diet**

    This is where we come in. The Whole-Food Vegan diet is based around a wide variety of whole foods such as seeds, nuts, legumes, whole grains, vegetables, and fruits. You will find that many of the delicious recipes in this book include foods from the list above. While you may think that you will be limited when you become vegan, you will need to open your mind to all of the incredible possibilities!

What to Eat

If you are just getting started with the vegan diet, the food restrictions may come across pretty daunting. Essentially, you will be limiting your food choices to plant-based foods. Luckily, there is a very long list of foods that you will be able to eat while following this diet. Below, we will go over some of the foods that you can include on your diet—so you go into your vegan journey, full of knowledge!

Vegetables and Fruits

Obviously, fruits and vegetables are going to be very high on your list. At this point in your life, you are most likely familiar with preparing some of your favorite dishes in a certain way. It should be noted that on the vegan diet, all dairy products such as buttermilk, cream, yogurt, butter, cheese, and milk are going to be eliminated. With that being said, there are some incredible alternatives such as coconut and soy. It will take a little bit of time to adjust, but you may find that you enjoy these alternatives even more—especially because they are going to be better for your health!

There will be many vegetables you can consume on the vegan diet. It will be important for you to learn how to balance your choices so you can consume all of the nutrients you need. Within this chapter, you will be provided with a list of high-protein foods—but you will also need to consume foods such as kale, broccoli, and bok choy to help with calcium levels.

Seeds, Nuts, and Legumes

As noted earlier, protein is going to be important once you remove animal products from your diet. The good news is that legumes are a wonderful plant-based and low-fat product for vegans to get their protein. You will be eating plenty of beans such as peanuts, pinto beans, split peas, black beans, lentils, and even chickpeas. There are unlimited ways to consume these foods in a number of different dishes.

You will also be eating plenty of seeds and nuts. Both of these foods help provide a proper amount of protein and healthy fats when consumed in moderation. It should be noted that nuts are typically high in calories, so if you are looking to lose weight while following the vegan lifestyle, you will have to limit your portions. These foods should also be consumed without salt or sweeteners for added health benefits.

Whole Grains

Another food that will be enjoyed while following a Vegan diet is whole-grains! There are a number of products you will be able to enjoy such as wild rice, rye, quinoa, oats, millet, barley, bulgur, and brown rice! You can include these foods in any meal whether it be breakfast, lunch, or dinner! It should be noted that you will need to change how you serve some of your favorite foods. You will have to say goodbye to any animal-based products and instead, try to include more vegetables and olive oil. You can still have your morning oatmeal, but you'll have to make the switch to almond or soy milk.

Vegan Food Products and Substitutions

On the modern market, you will see a number of vegan-friendly products that have been manufactured. Some of these products include vegan mayo, whipped cream, "meat" patties, and other frozen foods. While these are great to have on hand, they are still processed foods. You will want to be careful of foods that have added sugar and salts. Any excessive additives will undo the incredible benefits the vegan diet has to offer. While, of course, they are always an option, you should try your best to stick with whole foods.

Foods to Avoid

Poultry, Meat, and Seafood

Obviously, this is a given. These foods include quail, duck, goose, turkey, chicken, wild meat, organ meat, horse, veal, pork, lamb, and beef. An easy rule you can follow is that if it has a face or a mother, leave it out. You will also have to leave out any type of fish or seafood. These include lobster, crab, mussels, calamari, scallops, squid, shrimp, anchovies, and any fish.

Dairy and Eggs

Removing dairy and eggs from a diet is typically one of the hardest parts of becoming a vegan. When you are unable to put your favorite creamer into your coffee, or simply make a batch of brownies because you have to use eggs, you will begin to notice the major difference. If you wish to become vegan, you will have to find alternatives for ice cream, cream, butter, cheese, yogurt, milk, and any type of egg.

Animal-Based Ingredients

Animal-based ingredients are where you will have to be careful. I suggest learning how to read food labels so you can watch for tricky ingredients. You will want to avoid ingredients such as shellac, isinglass, carmine, cochineal, gelatin, egg white albumen, lactose, casein, and whey. You will also be avoiding animal-derived vitamin D3 as well as fish-derived omega-3 fatty acids.

Best Protein Sources

As noted earlier, one of the major concerns of a vegan diet is that it lacks sufficient amounts of proteins. With that being said, there are certain plant foods that not only provide vegans with proteins but a significant amount of protein. When you follow a high-protein diet, this can help with weight loss, satiety, and muscle strength. Below, you will find seventeen incredible plant-based foods that will provide you with the protein you need.

1. **Fruits and Vegetables**

   While all of the fruits and vegetables you will be eating on this diet contain protein, there are some that contain more protein than others. The vegetables you will want to look for include Brussel sprouts, sweet potatoes, potatoes, artichokes, asparagus, spinach, and broccoli. These vegetables contain about four to five grams of protein per cup that has been cooked. As for your fruits, you can try bananas, nectarines, blackberries, mulberries, cherimoyas, and guava. These fruits have two to four grams of protein per cup. If you are looking to add some extra protein into your diet, these are all excellent choices.

2. **Seeds, Nuts, and Nut Butters**

   As noted earlier, nuts and seeds are high in healthy fats and calories. They are also an excellent source of protein if you need to supplement extra food into your diet. One ounce of any nut or seed will typically contain anywhere from five to seven grams of protein! On top of this benefit, they are also great for B vitamins, vitamin E, phosphorus, selenium, magnesium, calcium, and iron depending on the variety you are consuming. When you are choosing your seeds and nuts, you will want to try to buy raw and unbalanced versions when possible. Also, keep a look out for natural nut butter that contains no added salt, sugar, and oil. Seeds and nuts are typically an easy way to consume the vitamins, minerals, and proteins you need while following a Vegan diet.

3. **Chia Seeds**

   At six grams of protein and thirteen grams of fiber per thirty-five grams, chia seeds are an excellent source of protein! Chia seeds are derived from a plant that is native to Guatemala and Mexico known as the Salvia Hispanica plant. These tiny seeds also contain antioxidants, omega-3 fatty acids, magnesium, selenium, calcium, and iron! The best part is that these seeds are very versatile. While they have a bland taste alone, they absorb water fairly easy and turn into a gel-like substance. You will find later in this book; chia seeds are used in a variety of recipes from chia puddings to baked goods and even in your smoothies!

4. Wild Rice

Wild rice is an important source of protein as it contains almost twice as much protein compared to other long-grain rice such as basmati and brown rice. If you were to cook one cup of wild rice, it would contain seven grams of protein! Along with this, wild rice also contains B vitamins, phosphorus, copper, magnesium, and a good amount of fiber. The best part is that wild rice is not stripped of its bran, unlike white rice. Bran contains vitamins, minerals, and fiber you will need while following the vegan diet. The only concern you may have about wild rice is arsenic. It has been found that arsenic accumulates in rice crops when it is grown in polluted areas. To avoid excessive arsenic consumption, you will want to wash wild rice and boil it before enjoying your meal.

5. Oatmeal and Oats

Welcome to your new favorite breakfast! Oats are a wonderful and delicious way to help get some extra protein into your diet. Half a cup of dry oats will provide you with about six grams of protein and four grams of fiber! While oats are not considered a complete protein, they have a high-quality protein, and they can be used in a number of different recipes. One of the more popular ways to include oats into your diet is to grind the oats into the flour so that you can use them for baking. Oats also include folate, phosphorus, zinc, and magnesium for added health benefits!

6. Soy Milk

As a vegan, you will be saying goodbye to any dairy products. Luckily, soy milk is an excellent alternative. Soy milk is made from soybeans and is often fortified with the minerals and vitamins your body needs to thrive. On top of this, soy milk also contains seven grams of proteins per cup, vitamin B12, vitamin D, and calcium! This product can be used in a number of different baking and cooking recipes, as you will be finding out later in this book. It should be noted that B12 is not naturally occurring in soybeans, so you should try to buy a fortified variety of soy milk. With that in mind, you will also want to opt for unsweetened soy milk. This way, you will be able to keep your added sugar levels low.

7. Sprouted Grains and Ezekiel Bread

While you will be able to eat bread as per usual, Ezekiel bread is an excellent alternative if you are looking to add more protein into your diet. This bread is made from legumes and sprouted whole grains such as soybeans, spelt, barley, millet, and wheat. In two slices of this bread, you will be provided with eight grams of protein. Sprouting grains typically increase the bread's beta-carotene content, vitamin E, vitamin C, folate, and soluble fiber. By consuming a healthier bread, it can help enhance digestion if you happen to be sensitive to gluten.

8. Quinoa and Amaranth

Both quinoa and amaranth will provide you with eight to nine grams of protein per cooked cup. These foods contain complete sources of protein which is fairly rare among grains. Oftentimes, quinoa and amaranth are referred to as gluten-free grains due to the fact that they do not grow from the grass like some other cereal grains. On top of these benefits, quinoa and amaranth are also excellent for added magnesium, phosphorus, manganese, iron, fiber, and complex carbs. These two foods can be prepared and consumed much as you would with any traditional grain, making them easy to add protein to your diet when needed.

9. Spirulina

Spirulina is a blue-green alga that is known as a nutritional powerhouse. With just two tablespoons of this food, you will be provided with potassium, manganese, riboflavin, magnesium, and eight grams of complete protein. Two tablespoons provide you with twenty-two percent of your dairy required thiamin and iron, as well and forty-two percent of your daily copper! It is also thought that spirulina has added benefits that can help improve blood sugar levels, cholesterol levels, reduce blood pressure, and can help build a stronger immune system.

10. Green Peas

You know the vegetable you probably pushed around your plate as a kid? It contains nine grams of protein per cup! A cup of peas alone has more protein than a cup of milk provides! On top of this much protein, peas also provide you with more than twenty-five percent of your daily manganese, folate, thiamine, vitamin A, vitamin C, vitamin K, and fiber. While green peas make an excellent side dish, they can be used in a number of different recipes. Whether you are making pea soup or stuffed ravioli, there is always room for more peas!

11. Hempseed

While hemp seed does derive from Cannabis sativa, a member of the marijuana plant family, hempseed only contains trace amounts of THC. This means that you cannot get high from consuming hemp seeds. However, these seeds do contain ten grams of protein per ounce! That is about fifty percent more protein compared to flaxseeds and chia seeds. On top of this excellent amount of protein, you will also be consuming a good amount of selenium, zinc, calcium, iron, magnesium, omega-3 and omega-6 fatty acids. It also believed that the fats in hemp seeds could help reduce inflammation and may help with symptoms that are involved with menopause and PMS. The best part is that hemp seeds are very easy to include in your diet. You can sprinkle the seeds on just about anything including home-made protein bars, salad dressings, and even in your morning smoothie!

12. Teff and Spelt

Teff and Spelt are other foods that belong in the ancient grain category. One of the differences between these two foods is that spelt contains gluten and teff is gluten-free. Both of these contain ten to eleven grams of protein per cup that is cooked. They are both also excellent sources of manganese, phosphorus, magnesium, iron, fiber, complex carbs, selenium, zinc, and B vitamins. If you are looking for a wheat and rice alternative, teff and spelt are an excellent option. They can be used in recipes for polenta, risotto, and even some baked goods.

13. Nutritional Yeast

You may have seen nutritional yeast in the store as yellow flakes or powder. Nutritional yeast comes from Saccharomyces cerevisiae yeast and has a cheesy flavor. This is a very popular ingredient if you are looking to creates meals such as scrambled tofu, mashed potatoes, or cheesy popcorn! In one ounce, you will be provided with seven grams of fiber and fourteen grams of protein! On top of the excellent protein source, nutritional yeast also contains B12, manganese, copper, magnesium, and zinc. If you are missing cheese in your life, you will want to get some nutritional yeast in your house.

14. Chickpeas and Beans

Chickpeas and beans such as pinto, black, and kidney beans all contain a lot of protein. In general, your bean varieties will contain about fifteen grams of protein for each cup you cook. They are also rich in manganese, potassium, phosphorus, folate, iron, fiber and complex carbs you need in your daily diet. With this being said, it is thought that a diet that is rich in beans can help reduce belly fat, lower blood pressure, decrease cholesterol, and may help control blood sugar levels. Luckily, there are a number of ways to add protein-packed legumes into your diet. From a side dish to homemade chili, you will find there are a number of different ways to enjoy beans!

15. Lentils

Lentils are another excellent source of protein! In one cup, you will receive eighteen grams of protein! The best part is that lentils can be used in a number of dishes from soups to salads! Lentils have slow-digested carbs and offer fifty percent of your daily fiber intake. The fiber found in lentils is excellent for a healthy gut and a healthy colon. All in all, lentils are another nutritional powerhouse. They offer the protein you need as well as iron, manganese, and folate!

16. Edamame, Tempeh, and Tofu

These foods all originate from soybeans. In general, soybeans are looked at as a whole source of protein. With that being said, this means that edamame, tempeh, and tofu all provide you with the essential amino acids that your body needs. Edamame has a sweet but slightly grassy taste. In general, you will want to boil or steam them before you consume them. Edamame is excellent for any soups or salads you may be making. Tofu, on the other hand, is excellent because it doesn't have much flavor! Due to the flavorless nature, it will easily absorb any ingredient it is prepared with. Tempeh typically has a nutty flavor. Both tempeh and tofu are excellent when you are making chili, soup, and even burgers! As you will find within the recipe chapters of this book, you will be cooking with tofu and tempeh often.

17. Seitan

Last but not least, you have seitan. Seitan is a very popular source of protein for both vegans and vegetarians. This particular food is made from gluten, making it resemble the texture of meat when it is being cooked. Seitan generally contains about twenty-five grams of protein per one hundred grams. With that being said, seitan is the richest plant protein you will be able to find. This food is also an excellent source of selenium, phosphorus, calcium, and iron. Seitan is very versatile as it can be grilled, sautéed, and pan-fried. If you have celiac disease or gluten sensitivity, you will want to avoid seitan due to the wheat gluten.

As you can see, there is no reason any vegetarian or vegan should have a protein deficiency. The key is knowing what to eat and where to get your nutrients from. With this information in hand, it will make it much easier when you are trying to prepare your meals for the day. If you feel you are lacking protein, or are unsatisfied with the protein source, there are always other options!

Primary Protein Functions

Protein is an incredibly important substance that can be found in every cell of your body. Aside from water, protein happens to be the most abundant substance in your body! The reason protein is so important in your diet is due to the fact that your body needs this protein for different vital processes. By consuming a proper diet, filled with protein, you will be able to help yourself out in a number of different ways.

1. **Antibodies**

Protein is the resource that forms antibodies within your immune system. With the proper number of antibodies, you will be able to prevent disease, illness, and infections. The proteins you consume are able to identify and destroy antigens like viruses and bacteria that enter your system. These proteins also work with the other cells in your immune system.

2. **Storage and Transportation of Molecules**

   Protein is also one of the major elements of molecule transportation. An example of this would be hemoglobin. Hemoglobin is the protein that helps transport oxygen around your body. Protein can also be used to help store molecules such as Ferritin. Ferritin is the protein that combines with iron and is stored in your liver.

3. **Enzymes**

   The enzymes within your body are proteins that are in charge of the chemical reactions in your body. One of the most familiar chemical reactions you are probably familiar with is destining! Without the proper amount of proteins, you would not be able to process carbohydrate and fat molecules into smaller molecules.

4. **Hormones**

   Another process that protein is important for is the creation of hormones. Hormones help control several body functions involving your organs. One small protein you may know is Insulin. Insulin is the hormone that helps you regulate your blood sugars. Another protein is secretin. Secretin is the substance that helps you digest by stimulating your pancreas and intestine so your body can create digestive juices.

5. **Energy**

   Energy is very important to get us through our daily activities. You guessed it; protein is a major source of energy! As you consume more protein, your body will be able to use this substance to help with body tissue maintenance and other functions. When the protein is not needed to intake other energy sources, protein can be stored as fat cells.

6. Maintenance and Repair

Protein is often known as the building block of the body. This is due to the fact that protein is vital when one is trying to maintain and repair their body tissue. Your organs, muscles, eyes, skin, and hair are all made from protein. This is why protein is very important in any diet you choose to follow.

7. Muscular Health

As you know, protein is present in all of your muscle tissue in the form of microfilaments; this is why it plays such an important role in the contraction and coordination of your muscles. As you include more protein in your diet, it will be important to create a balance between the rate of muscle protein synthesis you have and the breakdown of the muscle proteins. Essentially, this means that you will require different amounts of protein given your age and strength.

8. Improved Bone Health

Collagen is a protein in your body that helps provide structural scaffolding in your cells. This collagen is also vital if you are looking to sustain bone health. If you are an individual who exercises on a regular basis or are an athlete, protein will help keep your bones and muscles strong and healthy.

How Much Protein?

As you can tell, consuming protein is going to be extremely important, if you wish to live as healthy as possible. It will also be important that you learn how to balance your nutrients while providing enough protein on a vegan diet. The recommended daily protein requirement will change depending on your age and your health. It seems as though two to three servings of foods that are rich in protein is good enough for most adults. As a basic guide, women should shoot for .75 grams of protein per kilogram, and men should strive for .84 grams per kilogram. This number will change for a number of factors including individuals who are weight trainers, athletes, lactating, pregnant, or older.

Protein Deficiency

If you are following the vegan diet and are lacking an adequate amount of protein, you will feel the difference. It will be important to consume protein-rich foods due to the fact that your body does not store it. If you lack protein, you will place your body at risk of protein deficiency. Some of the side effects that you may experience include shrinking of muscle tissue, anemia, and fluid retention. If you experience any of these, please consult with your doctor to check for protein deficiency.

Side Effects from Protein

Much like with anything, there is such thing as too much of a good thing. If you consume too much protein, there are also some side effects that you may experience.

1. **Weight Gain**

   When you are following a vegan diet, balance is going to be key. Oftentimes, when individuals are attempting to lose weight, they will follow a high-protein and low-carb diet. When you are following this rule but not tracking your calorie intake, this could cause amino acids to convert into fatty acids, leading to weight gain. If you are focused on protein alone, this could lead to a deficiency in other nutrients your body needs.

2. **Cardiovascular Issues**

   While proteins do help with your muscles and tissue, too much protein could aggravate certain conditions such as high cholesterol and heart disease. This is why finding a balance with your carbohydrates, fats, and proteins are going to be important.

3. **Bone Health**

   As you learned earlier, protein is very important for bone health. However, it will be important you consume a proper amount of calcium to work alongside the protein. For some individuals, a high-protein diet can lead to an increase of urinary calcium which could potentially lead to bone resorption.

4. **Ammonia**

   Ammonia comes from protein metabolism and can be very hazardous for the body. This is the reason that the body will naturally convert ammonia into urea. This urea is then accumulated in your kidneys and then flushed from your body through urine. If you have an excess amount of protein, this can strain your kidneys as it tries to detoxify your body.

With all of that being said, you now know that protein is a very important part of your diet. While some naysayers may state that a vegan diet doesn't have enough protein, this couldn't be further from the truth. Now that you have a thorough understanding of proteins and the foods that you can consume, it is time to get to the cooking!

Chapter Two: Breakfast Recipes

    Breakfast is a very important meal. By starting your day off on the right foot, you will be that much closer to consuming your recommended nutrients such as vitamin D, B vitamins, iron, and protein! If you think skipping breakfast will help you lose weight, you are dead wrong. In a <u>study</u> done on children, the ones who skipped breakfast typically had a higher waist circumference and BMI. These children were also at higher risk of obesity and insulin issues. Within this chapter, you will be provided with a number of delicious vegan recipes for breakfast that are packed with protein!

Leek, Mushroom, and Spinach Breakfast Scramble

Time: Thirty-five Minutes

Servings: Four

Ingredients:

- Baby Spinach (6 Oz.)
- Red Pepper Flakes (.25 t.)
- Turmeric (.25 t.)
- Black Pepper (.25 t.)
- Sea Salt (.25 t.)
- Cumin (.50 t.)
- All-purpose Seasoning (1 t.)
- Nutritional Yeast (2 T.)
- Extra-firm Tofu (14 Oz.)
- Mushrooms (12)
- Leeks (2)
- Tomato (1)
- Black Olives (.25 C.)
- Olive Oil (1 t.)

Directions:

1. To begin this recipe, you will want to place a large skillet over a medium to high heat. Once the pan is warm, place the leeks in with a pinch of salt and cook until the leeks begin to brown. You will want to stir often to

assure that the leeks do not stick to the bottom of the pan.

2. Once the leeks are cooked through, add in the chopped mushrooms and cook for another five minutes or so.
3. With your vegetables being all set, crumble in your firm tofu. With the tofu in place, you will want to sprinkle your seasonings and nutritional yeast into the pan. You can give all of the ingredients a good stir to assure the tofu and vegetables are coated evenly.
4. Finally, add in the spinach and cook everything together for a minute or two. By the end, the spinach should be hot and wilted.
5. While serving, feel free to top off your tofu scramble with chopped tomatoes and black olives for some extra flavor profile!

Nutrition Values:

Calories: 180

Protein: 15g

Fat: 8g

Carbs: 18g

Fibers: 5g

Southwest Breakfast Tacos

Time: Thirty-five Minutes

Servings: Four

Ingredients:

- Black Beans (1 Can)
- Curry Powder (.25 t.)
- Black Pepper (.25 t.)
- Salt (.75 t.)
- Garlic (.50 t.)
- Ground Cumin (1.50 t.)
- Paprika (1.50 t.)
- Extra-firm Tofu (14 Oz.)
- Red Onion (.50 C.)
- Green Bell Pepper (.50)
- Red Bell Pepper (.50)
- Olive Oil (3 t.)
- Corn Tortillas
- Optional: Cilantro, Salsa, Scallions

Directions:

1. Before you begin cooking, you will want to prepare all of your vegetables. Please take the time now to dice your red onion, green bell pepper, and red bell pepper.

2. Once this is done, you will want to take a large pan and place it over medium heat. As the pan begins to warm up, place a teaspoon of olive oil and add in the diced vegetables. When the vegetables are in place, cook them for around five minutes or until they are tender.

3. When the vegetables are done, slide them to the side of the pan, so you have room to place the rest of your olive oil. When the olive oil is sizzling, add in your tofu and spices. Stir all of the ingredients in the pan together and cook until the tofu begins to brown. Typically, this will take ten to fifteen minutes.

4. Finally, you will want to add in your black beans. If you are not a fan of black beans, you can use any bean you enjoy! Cook all of the ingredients for another two minutes or until the beans are cooked through.

5. When you are ready, you can enjoy the tofu scramble alone or enjoy it in a breakfast taco. For more flavor, try adding salsa, cilantro, or green onions!

Nutrition Values:

Calories: 340

Protein: 25g

Fat: 13g

Carbs: 37g

Fibers: 13g

Black Bean and Sweet Potato Breakfast Burrito

Time: Forty Minutes

Servings: Four

Ingredients:

- Tortillas (4)
- Black Beans (1 Can)
- Spinach (2 C.)
- Cumin (2 t.)
- Nutritional Yeast (1 T.)
- Silken Tofu (1 Package)
- Green Chili (6 Oz.)
- Green Onions (3)
- Mushrooms (8)
- Olive Oil (4 T.)
- Sweet Potato (1)
- Pepper (.50 t.)
- Salt (.50 t.)
- Optional: Salsa

Directions:

1. To begin, you will want to prepare your sweet potatoes by cutting them into small cubes. You can also prepare your green onions by slicing the white and the green parts into thin pieces.

2. When the vegetables are prepared, go ahead and heat your oven to 375 degrees.

3. As the oven heats up, you will want to take a baking sheet and carefully place the cubed sweet potato. Once in place, drizzle two tablespoons of olive oil over the top and sprinkle with your salt and pepper. When ready, place the baking sheet in the oven for thirty-five to forty minutes. By the end, the potatoes should be nice and tender.

4. When the sweet potato is cooking in the oven, you can begin cooking your green onion and mushrooms in a pan over medium heat. You will only need to cook these for three to five minutes for the mushrooms to become nice and tender.

5. Once the mushrooms are cooked through, add in the cumin, nutritional yeast, green chili, and silken tofu. Be sure to mix all of the ingredients around to assure even coating. Cook all of these for another three to five minutes. At this point, the tofu should be warm.

6. Finally, toss the spinach into the pan and cook until the spinach begins to wilt. During this time, feel free to season with salt and pepper as needed. When all of these ingredients are cooked through, set it to the side and return the pan to the heat. In the same pan, you can begin to heat your black beans. At this point, your sweet potato should be ready!

7. When the sweet potatoes are cooked through, remove the pan from the oven and allow to cool. When the pieces are safe to handle, begin to assemble your burritos by layering your potatoes, beans, and tofu mixture. Wrap and serve for a delicious, protein-rich breakfast!

Nutrition Values:

Calories: 520

Protein: 17g

Fat: 20g

Carbs: 71g

Fibers: 14g

Tofu Scramble Burrito Bowl

Time: Forty Minutes

Servings: Two

Ingredients:

- Cilantro (2 T.)
- Avocado (.25 C.)
- Salsa (.25 C.)
- Black Pepper (.25 t.)
- Salt (.25 t.)
- Spinach (2 C.)
- Black Beans (.50 C.)
- Bell Pepper (1 C.)
- Red Onion (.75 C.)
- Black Salt (.50 t.)
- Ground Turmeric (.25 t.)
- Nutritional Yeast (2 T.)
- Extra-firm Tofu (1 Package)
- Cooking Oil (2 T.)

Directions:

1. To begin, you will want to slice your onion and bell peppers into strips. Once this is done, begin to heat a large pan over medium heat. When it is hot, carefully use your hands to break the tofu apart and cook for

three minutes. Be sure to stir the tofu around, so it browns on all sides.

2. Once the tofu is cooked through, you will want to turn down the heat and add in the black salt, turmeric, and nutritional yeast. If desired, you can also add salt and pepper for extra flavor.

3. When the tofu is perfectly browned, go ahead and add in the red onion and bell peppers. You will want to sauté this mix until the onion becomes translucent. Once the onions and bell peppers are cooked through, add in the spinach and beans.

4. To assemble your burrito bowl, divide the tofu scramble and vegetables into two bowls. For extra flavor, you can try to add cilantro, avocado, or even salsa!

Nutrition Values:

Calories: 290

Protein: 11g

Fat:17g

Carbs: 27g

Fibers: 12g

Chickpea Breakfast Enchiladas

Time: One Hour

Servings: Ten

Ingredients:

- Corn Tortillas (10)
- Liquid Smoke (.25 t.)
- Agave Nectar (2 t.)
- Adobo Sauce (3 T.)
- Chipotle Pepper in Adobo Sauce (1)
- Tomato Puree (24 Oz.)
- Dried Oregano (.25 t.)
- Garlic Powder (.25 t.)
- Ground Black Pepper (.25 t.)
- Paprika (.25 t.)
- Chickpeas (15 Oz.)
- Jalapeno (1)
- Bell Pepper (1)
- White Onion (.50)
- Russet Potato (1)
- Olive Oil (1 T.)
- Optional: Red Onion, Fresh Cilantro, Guacamole, Chipotle Sauce, Chickpeas

Directions:

1. To begin this recipe, you will first want to make the chickpea scramble filling. You can do this by first heating a medium-sized skillet over medium heat. Once it is warm, add in the olive oil and the cubed potato. To cook, be sure you frequently stir for eight minutes.

2. When the potatoes are cooked through, you will want to add in the onion, bell peppers, jalapeno, and all of the ground spices. Go ahead and cook all of these ingredients together until the potato is fully cooked.

3. As the vegetables cook, you will want to prepare your chickpeas by adding a whole can into your food processor. Once in place, blend the chickpeas until they reach a smooth consistency. When you are ready, pour the chickpeas into the hot skillet and cook for two to four minutes. As the tofu becomes firm, gently fold all of the ingredients together.

4. With the scramble part done, it is time to make your chipotle sauce. All you need to do for this is warm up a tablespoon of olive oil in a saucepan over medium heat. Once the oil begins to sizzle, add in the oregano, garlic, black pepper, and the paprika. You will want to go ahead and cook this for thirty seconds. Once this is done, add in the liquid smoke, agave nectar, adobo sauce, chipotle pepper, and the tomato puree. Be sure to stir everything together well, so it combines evenly. Once it begins to bubble, set the sauce to the side.

5. Now, you will want to heat your oven to 375 degrees. As the oven heats up, take a small casserole dish and place a few ladles of sauce into the bottom.

6. Next, you will want to take your corn tortillas and gently fill them with the chickpea mixture from before. When they are filled, you will want to roll them and place them seam-side down int your casserole dish. Once this step is complete, spoon the rest of the sauce over the top.
7. With your enchiladas in place, pop them into the oven for twenty minutes or until cooked through.
8. For added flavor, you can serve your meal with any of your vegan-friendly toppings!

Nutrition Values:

Calories: 190

Protein: 6g

Fat: 4g

Carbs: 33g

Fibers: 5g

Quinoa with Tempeh

Time: Forty Minutes

Servings: Six

Ingredients:

- Nutritional Yeast (1 T.)
- Maple Syrup (1 T.)
- Nutmeg (.25 t.)
- Cayenne Pepper (.25 t.)
- Dried Thyme (.50 t.)
- Dried Sage (1 t.)
- Garlic Powder (.50 t.)
- Vegetable Oil (1 T.)
- Water (.50 C.)
- Salt (.50 t.)
- Tempeh (8 Oz.)
- Soy Sauce (1 T.)
- Sesame Oil (1 t.)
- Spinach (2 C.)
- Vegetable Broth (2 C.)
- Quinoa (1 C.)

Directions:

1. To start this recipe, you are going to cook your quinoa. All you are going to have to do is place the quinoa with

two cups of vegetable broth into a large saucepan. Once in place, bring the mixture to a boil and place a cover on the saucepan. Allow this mixture to cook for about fifteen minutes or until all of the liquid is gone. When the quinoa is cooked, remove from the pan and place to the side.

2. Next, you are going to want to place your oil into the cleared pan and begin to cook your spinach. Once the spinach begins to wilt, you will then add the soy sauce. Cook this mixture for two to three minutes and then toss the spinach mixture with your cooked quinoa.

3. Finally, it is time to make tempeh. To prepare the tempeh, slice it into bite-sized pieces and place in frying pan with a half teaspoon of water. Allow the tempeh to cook until the water has evaporated. You can coat tempeh with just about any seasoning that you enjoy. For this recipe, we have chosen to use cayenne pepper, thyme, sage, garlic powder, maple syrup, and nutritional yeast. When the tempeh is cooked through, add it to the quinoa and spinach mixture. Serve warm and enjoy your savory breakfast!

Nutrition Values:

Calories: 230

Protein: 12g

Fat: 9g

Carbs: 26g

Fibers:3g

Coconut Split Pea Breakfast Porridge Bowl

Time: Fifty Minutes

Servings: Five

Ingredients:

- Brown Rice, Cooked (4 C.)
- Lime Juice (1 T.)
- Coconut Milk (.50 C.)
- Water (4 C.)
- Yellow Split Peas (1.50 C.)
- Black Pepper (.25 t.)
- Salt (.25 t.)
- Coriander (.50 t.)
- Cumin (.50 t.)
- Turmeric (1 t.)
- Minced Ginger (2 t.)
- Small Carrots (2)
- Yellow Onion (1)
- Mustard Seeds (1 t.)
- Coconut Oil (1 T.)

Directions:

1. To start this recipe, you will want to take a medium-sized pot and place it over medium heat. As the pot begins to warm up, place the coconut oil and mustard

seeds. Allow these to cook until the seeds begin to pop. At this point, you will want to add in your carrots and onions. Allow the vegetables to cook for eight to ten minutes, or until they become soft.

2. When the vegetables are cooked through, add in a couple of tablespoons of water. Once in place, gently stir in the pepper, salt, coriander, cumin, turmeric, and the ginger. When you begin to smell the spices, add in the extra water and split peas so you can bring everything to a boil. Once boiling, reduce your heat to a simmer and cover the pot.

3. You will be cooking this mixture for thirty-five to forty minutes. By the end of this time, the split peas should be nice and tender. You will want to stir the split peas multiple times as they cook, to assure they do not stick to the bottom of the pot. If the peas become thick, you can add in more water as needed.

4. When the split peas are finally cooked through, carefully add in the lime juice and the coconut milk. You should feel free to season with extra salt, pepper, and turmeric to your liking. Finally, serve your meal with rice and any toppings of your choice.

Nutrition Values:

Calories: 280

Protein: 10g

Fat: 10g

Carbs: 44g

Fibers: 5g

Chickpea Pancakes

Time: Thirty Minutes

Servings: Five

Ingredients:

- Flax Meal (.25 C.)
- Chickpea Flour (2 C.)
- Spinach (3 C.)
- Tomatoes (1 C.)
- Bell Pepper (1 C.)
- Red Onion (.25 C.)
- Oil (As Needed)
- Ground Cayenne Pepper (.10 t.)
- Pepper (.10 t.)
- Onion Powder (.25 t.)
- Garlic Powder (.25 t.)
- Salt (.25 t.)
- Water (.50 C.)
- Avocado (.50)
- Unsweetened Almond Milk (1.50 C.)
- Ground Cayenne Pepper (1 t.)
- Turmeric (.25 t.)
- Onion Powder (.50 t.)

- Garlic Powder (.50 t.)
- Salt (1 t.)
- Baking Powder (2.50 t.)
- Nutritional Yeast (3 T.)

Directions:

1. If you are looking to add an extra serving of vegetables to your day, this first step is completely optional. To begin, heat a medium pan over medium heat and place a teaspoon of oil. Once the pan is hot, toss in chopped onion, bell peppers, and tomatoes. Be sure to stir to combine well and cook through until the vegetables begin to soften. Finally, add in spinach and cook until it is slightly wilted. Once the vegetables are cooked, place them off to the side.

2. Now, take a large bowl and mix together the cayenne pepper, turmeric, pepper, onion powder, garlic powder, salt, baking powder, nutritional yeast, flax meal, and the chickpea flour. Be sure to stir well to assure all of the ingredients are well combined.

3. Once you have the mixture from above, you will slowly want to pour in the milk. As you do this, stir to combine and add more liquid if you would like thinner pancakes. If you cooked the vegetables from above, add them into your batter.

4. With this set, carefully pour the batter onto a hot skillet and cook the pancakes for two to four minutes on either side. When the downside begins to brown, carefully flip the pancake and cook through on the other side. Cooking the other side of the pancake will typically only take about one to two minutes.

5. Now that your pancakes are done, you can make an avocado sauce to pour over the top. All you need to do is place cayenne pepper, pepper, onion powder, garlic powder, water, and avocado into a blender and churn until it is smooth.
6. Finally, top your pancakes and enjoy a delicious and healthy breakfast!

Nutrition Values:

Calories: 300

Protein: 15g

Fat: 14g

Carbs: 34g

Fibers: 12g

Falafel Waffles

Time: Forty Minutes

Servings: Two

Ingredients:

- Chickpea Flour (1 C.)
- Black Pepper (.25 t.)
- Salt (.50 t.)
- Cumin Powder (2 t.)
- Spinach (1 C.)
- Fresh Cilantro (.50 C.)
- Red Onion (1)
- Garlic (1)
- Chickpeas (.75 C.) NOTE: Soak Overnight

Directions:

1. Once your chickpeas have soaked in water overnight, you will want to place them into a blender and blend for a few seconds. When this step is complete, add all of the ingredients from above minus the flour and continue to blend. In the end, you will have a batter with a chunky texture.

2. Next, add in the flour and blend until the ingredients are well combined. Once this is done, pour the mixture into a bowl and place it in the fridge for about an hour.

3. After the time has passed, you will want to preheat your waffle maker. When ready, coat the waffle maker with a non-stick spray and pour some batter int the waffle maker. Once in place, cook according to the instructions and then enjoy!

Nutrition Values:

Calories: 360

Protein: 17g

Fat: 6g

Carbs: 61g

Fibers: 13g

Chia Zucchini Breakfast Muffins

Time: One Hour

Servings: Nine

Ingredients:

- Water (.10 C.)
- Sugar (.25 t.)
- Salt (.25 t.)
- Baking Powder (1 t.)
- Lemon Pepper (1 T.)
- Almond Flour (2 C.)
- Zucchini (3)
- Chia Seeds (2 T.) NOTE: Soak in .50 C. of Water

Directions:

1. To begin this recipe, you will want to place chopped zucchini pieces into a food processor and grind until it becomes watery and fine. When zucchini is ready, place it into a container and strain with the help of a cheesecloth. You will want to squeeze as much excess water out as possible. You will want to collect this water for later use.

2. Next, it is time to heat your oven to 350 degrees. As the oven warms up, you can also prepare your muffin tray by spraying it with your favorite non-stick spray.

3. When you are ready, take a large mixing bowl and combine the salt, baking powder, lemon pepper, and almond flour. Be sure to stir everything together well, so

the ingredients are spread evenly. With this in place, add in your zucchini pieces and soaked chia seeds. Last, pour in the zucchini water you saved from before.

4. Once all of the ingredients from above are combined well, it is time to scoop the batter into the muffin tray. When ready, place the muffin tray into your heated oven for forty-five to fifty minutes. By the end, the muffins should be cooked through and golden-brown on top. These are excellent to enjoy immediately or on the go.

Nutrition Values:

Calories: 150

Protein: 7g

Fat: 12g

Carbs: 8g

Fibers: 3g

Peanut Butter Protein Granola Bars

Time: Forty Minutes

Servings: Fourteen

Ingredients:

- Brown Rice Syrup (.50 C.)
- Peanut Butter (.75 C.)
- Unsalted Peanuts (.50 C.)
- Chia Seeds (2 T.)
- Rolled Oats (4 C.)

Directions:

1. To begin, you will need to preheat your oven to 350 degrees.

2. As the oven begins to warm up, you will want to take a large bowl and combine your unsalted peanuts, chia seeds, and oats. Once these are well combined, toss in the brown rice syrup and stir everything together.

3. The best part about granola bars is how easily customizable they are! If you have any add-ins, feel free to fold them into the dough as desired. It is possible you may need to use your hands and work the granola if it is too dry.

4. Once all of your ingredients are in place, add in melted peanut butter to get everything to stick together. If the granola is still too dry for your taste, feel free to add in extra peanut butter or syrup as needed.

5. When the mixture is ready, press the dough you have created into a baking dish. Pop this into the dish for

twenty-five minutes. If you don't have time to cook, this recipe can also be a no-bake granola bar. If you do not want to cook the granola, press the dough into your pan and place in the fridge for about sixty minutes.

Nutrition Values:

Calories: 230

Protein: 8g

Fat: 12g

Carbs: 27g

Fibers: 4g

Overnight Oats

Time: Five Minutes

Servings: One

Ingredients:

- Pecans (5)
- Unsweetened Soy Milk (1 C.)
- Maple Syrup (1 t.)
- Vanilla Plant-based Protein Powder (.50 Scoop)
- Chia Seeds (1 t.)
- Rolled Oats (.50 C.)

Directions:

1. Overnight Oats are easy and delicious! To begin, all you will need to do is place the soy milk, maple syrup, protein powder, chia seeds, and rolled oats into a bowl or mason jar. Once in place, be sure you give all of the ingredients a good stir to make sure they are well blended.
2. Once in place, pop the mason jar or bowl into your fridge overnight.
3. In the morning, sprinkle your choice of nut (I like Pecans!) over the top and enjoy! If you enjoy your oatmeal warm, you can always place the bowl into the microwave for a minute or so.

Nutrition Values:

Calories: 370

Protein: 14g

Fat: 20g

Carbs: 40g

Fibers: 8g

Spicy Breakfast Skillet

Time: One Hour

Servings: Four

Ingredients:

- Green Onion (2)
- Avocado (1)
- Cherry Grape Tomatoes (.50 C.)
- Potatoes (2)
- Sweet Potato (1)
- Black Beans (2 C.)
- Garlic (1)
- Ground Cumin (1 t.)
- Chili Powder (1 t.)
- Tempeh (4 Oz.)
- Grapeseed Oil (1 T.)
- Pepper (.50 t.)
- Salt (.50 t.)
- Non-dairy Cream (.50 C.)
- Garlic (1)
- Jalapeno Pepper (1)
- Optional: Hot Sauce, Tortillas, Cilantro

Directions:

1. To begin this recipe, we will be making the sauce that goes with this delicious and spicy breakfast skillet. First, you will want to place a medium to large skillet over a medium to high heat. Once the skillet begins to warm up, you will then add in one of the garlic cloves and chopped jalapenos. Go ahead and cook these two ingredients until they are browned on all sides.

2. Next, you will be transferring the garlic and jalapeno into the blender. Once in place, add in the pepper, salt, cilantro, lime juice, and your nut pod creamer. Now, all you will have to do is blend the ingredients until they are smooth. When the sauce is done, transfer it to a bowl and set to the side.

3. With the sauce done, it is time to get to the main event. First, you will preheat your oven to 400 degrees.

4. As the oven heats up, you will want to take the same skillet from above and place a tablespoon of your oil in it. Once the oil begins to sizzle, add in the chopped pieces of tempeh and stir. You will continue to stir the tempeh until it is well browned. Typically, this will take about four minutes.

5. Once the tempeh is cooked through, it is now time to add in your spices. Carefully add in the garlic, cumin, chili powder, and then cook for an additional thirty seconds.

6. When the spices become fragrant, it is time to add the black beans along with your salt and pepper. When the black beans are cooked through, turn your heat off and place this mixture into another bowl.

7. If you haven't already, you will want to take the time to chop your potatoes and sweet potatoes into small, bite-sized pieces. Once you have done this, place them into your heated skillet with the rest of your grapeseed oil. If desired, feel free to season the potatoes with salt and pepper. Once the potatoes are done, place them in a skillet and roast in the oven for thirty-five to forty minutes. In the end, the potatoes should be nice and tender.

8. After cooking all of your potatoes, remove them from the oven and gently stir in the black bean and tempeh mixture you made earlier. When everything is in place, feel free to decorate with your favorite toppings. For this recipe, I chose avocado and chopped tomatoes.

9. Finally, drizzle your jalapeno sauce over the top and enjoy on a nice, warm tortilla!

Nutrition Values:

Calories: 430

Protein: 17g

Fat: 16g

Carbs: 59g

Fibers: 15g

Vegan Omelet

Time: Thirty Minutes

Servings: One

Ingredients:

- Diced Onion (.25 C.)
- Diced Tomatoes (.25 C.)
- Diced Mushrooms (.25 C.)
- Spinach (.25 C.)
- Cornstarch (1 t.)
- Paprika (.25 t.)
- Black Pepper (.25 t.)
- Salt (.25 t.)
- Nutritional Yeast (2 T.)
- Minced Garlic (2)
- Hummus (2 T.)
- Firm Tofu (5 Oz.)
- Optional: Vegan Parmesan Cheese, Salsa, Fresh Herbs

Directions:

1. Before you begin cooking, you will want to heat your oven to 375 degrees. As the oven warms up, take the time now to prepare your vegetables by cutting them into small, bite-sized pieces. You will also want to press and drain your tofu, so it is ready to be cooked. When

this step is complete, you can place everything to the side.

2. Next, you will want to take a pan and place it over medium heat. When it is hot enough, carefully add in your garlic and olive oil. At this point, you will want to cook the garlic for two minutes or until it turns a golden-brown color.

3. Now, you can add the garlic, tofu, and cornstarch into a food processor. Blend on high until the ingredients are mixed together well. If needed, you may have to scrape the sides down. In the event that the ingredients are too thick, add in a tablespoon or two of water to help thin it. Once done, set the mixture to the side.

4. In the warm skillet from earlier, you will want to place a bit more olive oil. When the olive oil begins to sizzle, carefully add in the diced vegetables from before and begin to cook them. At this point, you can season the vegetables with salt and pepper to the desired flavor. You will want to cook the vegetables for five minutes or until they are nice and soft. Once this is complete, you can set these to the side.

5. Next, you will be removing the skillet from the heat. Before you begin cooking your omelet, be sure there is enough oil spread around so that it does not stick to the pan. When this is done, add in ¼ of the vegetables and spoon a part of the omelet batter into the pan. You will want to spread it out as evenly as possible, without creating any gaps or tears in the batter.

6. When everything is in place, turn up the heat to medium and cook the omelet for about five minutes. At this point, the edges should begin to look dry. Once this happens, place the skillet into the oven and bake until

the omelet is a golden-brown color. Typically, this will take anywhere from ten to fifteen minutes. The longer you bake it, the less soft the omelet will be.

7. In the last five minutes, carefully add the remaining vegetables on top of the omelet and cook for another one to two minutes. When everything is set, remove the omelet from the oven and allow to cool several minutes before you enjoy. For some extra flavor, you can add cilantro, vegan parmesan cheese, or even salsa!

Nutrition Values:

Calories: 280

Protein: 26g

Fat: 8g

Carbs: 35g

Fibers: 13g

Country Hash

Time: Forty-five Minutes

Servings: Four

Ingredients:

- Minced Garlic (2)
- Chopped Onion (1)
- Ground Turmeric (.125 t.)
- Black Salt (.25 t.)
- Nutritional Yeast (2 T.)
- Firm Tofu (14 Oz.)
- Vegan Butter (2 T.)
- Bay Leaf (1)
- Diced Russet Potatoes (1 Lb.)
- Ground Coriander (.10 t.)
- Dried Dill (.10 t.)
- Dried Oregano (.25 t.)
- Sea Salt (.75 t.)
- Dried Chives (2 t.)
- Black Eyed Peas (1 C.)
- Cayenne (.10 t.)
- Chopped Scallion (1)

Directions:

1. To start this recipe, you will first be cooking your potatoes. Before you begin cooking, you will want to dice your potato into half inch cubes. Once this step is complete, add the potatoes and your bay leaf into a saucepan with a small amount of water. When everything is in place, bring the pan to a boil and immediately turn the heat down and simmer the ingredients. At this point, you will want to cook the potatoes for five minutes. After this time, remove the saucepan from the heat, drain the water, and set everything to the side. You can discard the bay leaf, as it is no longer needed.

2. Next, you will want to take a small bowl and begin to mash your tofu. When the tofu is soft, add in the turmeric, salt, and the nutritional yeast. When this is done, set the bowl to the side

3. Next, you will be taking a large skillet and placing it over medium heat. As the pan begins to warm up, add in the chives, garlic, and the onion. You will want to cook this mixture for three minutes, or until soft. Once this is done, add in the potatoes and season with black pepper, coriander, dill, oregano, thyme, and salt. You can adjust the amounts of season used according to your own taste.

4. When everything is in place, be sure you stir, so nothing sticks to the bottom of the pan. You will want to cook everything together for ten minutes or so. If needed, add in two tablespoons of water to keep everything from burning.

5. When the potatoes are tender, stir in one tablespoon of your vegan butter. Once the butter has melted, add in the black-eyed peas and tofu. For extra flavor, try

seasoning the dish with black pepper, salt, and cayenne pepper. After a few minutes, a light crust should begin developing on the bottom. Now, flip portions of the hash until everything is heated through.

6. Finally, remove the dish from the heat, allow to cool, and enjoy. For extra flavor, try garnishing your dish with scallions.

Nutrition Values:

Calories: 320

Protein: 25g

Fat: 9g

Carbs: 40g

Fibers: 5g

Chapter Three: Lunch Recipes

Vegan Veggie Protein Burgers

Time: One Hour and Five Minutes

Servings: Three

Ingredients:

- Vital Wheat Gluten (.50 C.)
- Water (.25 C)
- Liquid Smoke (.10 t.)
- Paprika (.25 t.)
- Ground Chili (.25 t.)
- Garlic Powder (.25 t.)
- Onion Powder (.25 t.)
- Oregano (.25 t.)
- Ground Cumin (.50 t.)
- Soy Sauce (1 T.)
- Tomato Paste (1 T.)
- Maple Syrup (1 T.)
- Olive Oil (3 T.)
- Red Kidney Beans (.50 C.)
- Vegetable Protein of Choice (1 C.)

Directions:

1. To begin, you will want to bring a large pot of water to a boil. When the water is finally boiling, go ahead and place your vegetable protein of choice. Allow the protein to simmer for ten to twelve minutes to make sure it is cooked through. Once this time is finished, drain the protein and set it to the side.

2. Next, you will want to get your food processor out. Once in place, add in the water, liquid smoke, spices, nutritional yeast, soy sauce, tomato paste, maple syrup, oil, and cooked beans. You will want to process these ingredients together until it forms a puree texture.

3. Add in your vegetable protein and process everything together for another ten seconds. By the end, all of the ingredients should look like a Bolognese sauce. You will not want big chunks, as then your burger will not be held together well.

4. After preparing your burger, transfer the mixture over to a large mixing bowl. Once in place, add in the vital wheat gluten and begin to knead everything together so you can help develop the gluten. At the end of this, the mixture should be nice and soft.

5. With this step complete, take the mixture in your hands and form three patties. You can wrap the burgers in parchment paper and then fold into aluminum foil. If you do it this way, you can place the patties into an Instant Pot or Pressure Cooker for one hour and twenty minutes. Finally, remove from the tin foil and allow the burgers to cool for ten minutes. If you do not have an instant pot, you can also throw them onto the stove-top and cook until golden brown on each side.

6. Serve these burgers on your favorite rolls and topped with your favorite vegetables for a healthy and protein packed lunch!

Nutrition Values:

Calories: 260

Protein: 19g

Fat: 15g

Carbs:14g

Fibers: 2g

Vegan High-Protein Chili

Time: Forty Minutes

Servings: Four

Ingredients:

- Chopped Yellow Squash (1)
- Chopped Red Bell Pepper (1)
- Chopped Onion (3 T.)
- Olive Oil (1 T.)
- Vegan Ground Beef (1)
- Pepper (.25 t.)
- Salt (.25 t.)
- Cayenne (.25 t.)
- Chili Powder (.50 t.)
- Tomato Sauce (1 Can)
- Garlic (3)

Directions:

1. To begin your vegan chili, you will first want to prepare all of your ingredients from above. Carefully take all of the vegetables from the list above and chop them into small, bite-sized pieces.

2. When the vegetables are prepared, you will now want to take the bell pepper and onion and cook them in a pan over medium heat. I suggest cooking them for three to four minutes, or until they begin to soften. Once they are soft, you can add in the squash pieces and the garlic. If

desired, go ahead and season these vegetables with the cayenne and chili powder. Once in place, continue to cook all of the vegetables for another three to four minutes.

3. Finally, add in the tomato sauce and vegan ground beef. You will cook this mixture until everything is well heated. For extra flavor, you can add salt and pepper as desired. Enjoy with your favorite toppings for a delicious lunch. If the chili is too thick, feel free to add water or vegetable oil as needed.

Nutrition Values:

Calories: 370

Protein: 9g

Fat: 15g

Carbs: 52g

Fibers: 13g

Vegan Mexican Quinoa

Time: Thirty-five Minutes

Servings: Four

Ingredients:

- Cilantro Leaves (2 T.)
- Lime (1)
- Avocado (1)
- Black Pepper (.25 t.)
- Salt (.25 t.)
- Cumin (.50 t.)
- Chili Powder (1 t.)
- Corn Kernels (1 C.)
- Diced Tomatoes (1 Can)
- Black Beans (1 Can)
- Vegetable Broth (1 C.)
- Quinoa (1 C.)
- Jalapeno (1)
- Garlic (2)
- Olive Oil (1 T.)

Directions:

1. To start, you are going to want to put a large skillet over medium heat so you can begin to heat your olive oil. Once the olive oil is sizzling, go ahead and add in the jalapeno and garlic. Stir these two ingredients together for about a minute or until it becomes fragrant.

2. Once the jalapeno is cooked, you will want to add in the quinoa, corn, tomatoes, beans, and the vegetable broth. Once the broth begins to boil, add in the salt, pepper, cumin, and the chili powder. When the spices are in place, reduce the heat and allow the quinoa to cook through. Typically, this takes about twenty minutes or so.

3. Finally, add in the lime juice, avocado, and the cilantro. With the final touches, your lunch is ready to be enjoyed!

Nutrition Values:

Calories: 450

Protein: 23g

Fat: 14g

Carbs: 63g

Fibers: 16g

Protein Pasta Fagioli

Time: Thirty-five Minutes

Servings: Four

Ingredients:

- Elbow Pasta (6 Oz.)
- Water (2 C.)
- Vegetable Stock (4 C.)
- Parsley (2 T.)
- Basil (2 T.)
- Salt (.50 t.)
- Red Pepper Flakes (.25 t.)
- Black Pepper (1 t.)
- Bay Leaf (1)
- Tomato Sauce (1 Can)
- Cannellini Beans (30 Oz.)
- Carrots (1 C.)
- Onion (1 C.)
- Olive Oil (2 T.)

Directions:

1. To start, you will want to take a large pot and place your olive oil over medium heat. Once the olive oil is sizzling, you can sauté the carrots, onions, and garlic you have chopped into small pieces.

2. Once these vegetables are soft and cooked through, add in the water, vegetable stock, spices, tomato sauce, and beans. When the ingredients are in place, bring everything to a boil. Once boiling, reduce the heat and simmer everything for fifteen minutes or so.

3. Finally, add in the pasta and cook in the same pot uncovered until the pasta is cooked through according to their own directions. When the pasta is done, your dish is ready to be enjoyed!

Nutrition Values:

Calories: 520

Protein: 50g

Fat: 13g

Carbs: 63g

Fibers: 6g

Spicy Lentil Stew

Time: Forty Minutes

Servings: Six

Ingredients:

- Spinach Leaves (3 C.)
- Diced Tomatoes (1 Can)
- Red Lentils (1.50 C.)
- Vegetable Broth (4 C.)
- Cayenne Pepper (1 t.)
- Spice Blend (2 T.)
- Ginger (1.50 t.)
- Garlic Cloves (3)
- Onion (1)
- Olive Oil (2 T.)
- Salt (.25 t.)
- Pepper (.25 .t)

Directions:

1. First, you will want to take a large pot and place it over medium heat. As the pot begins to warm up, place the olive oil and begin to sauté your onion. Typically, this will take about five minutes. Once the onion is soft, add in the ginger, garlic, cayenne, and spice mix. Stir everything in the pot for another minute or so.

2. Next, you will want to add in diced potatoes, tomatoes, dry red lentils, and the vegetable broth. You will want to

stir everything together and then raise the heat so you can bring the pot to a simmer. Once everything is simmering, lower the heat and allow the lentils and potatoes to cook until they are soft and tender. This will usually take about thirty minutes or so.

3. When the potatoes and lentils are done, stir in the spinach and stir carefully until the spinach begins to wilt. Once this is done, remove the dish from the heat and season with salt and pepper as desired. Serve warm and enjoy!

Nutrition Values:

Calories: 310

Protein: 16g

Fat: 5g

Carbs: 51g

Fibers: 19g

Cauliflower and White Bean Alfredo Pasta

Time: One Hour

Servings: Four

Ingredients:

- Whole Grain Pasta (10 Oz.)
- Red Pepper Flakes (2 t.)
- Mushrooms (.50 C.)
- Sun-Dried Tomatoes (.25 t.)
- Kale Leaves (3)
- Nutritional Yeast (2 T.)
- Pepper (.25 t.)
- Salt (.25 t.)
- Nutmeg (.25 t.)
- Shallot (1)
- Olive Oil (2 T.)
- Unsweetened Almond Milk (1.25 C.)
- Cauliflower (.50)
- Cannellini Beans (1 Can)

Directions:

1. As for the first step, you will want to make your alfredo sauce. You will do this by cutting your cauliflower into large florets and then place it into a pot with boiling water. When the cauliflower is in place, cook it for about twenty minutes or until it is soft.

2. As the cauliflower cooks in the pot, you can take a pan and begin to heat it over medium heat. Once it is warm, add in your shallots and cook them until they are lightly browned.

3. After cooking these two ingredients, place them into a blender along with the nutmeg, milk, and beans. Blend everything together until you create a creamy texture. If desired, go ahead and flavor everything with pepper and salt. If you want, feel free to flavor with any of your favorite spices! If the sauce turns out too thick, you can always add in milk or water as needed.

4. Next, it is time to cook your vegetables! For this next step, you will need to take the same pan from before and heat one tablespoon of olive oil with medium heat. When the oil begins to sizzle, add in the mushrooms, tomatoes, kale, and red pepper flakes. Go ahead and sauté the kale f five minutes or so. When you are done, remove the vegetables from the pan and set to the side.

5. Finally, you will want to cook your pasta according to the package.

6. With all of your ingredients cook and ready, it is time to assemble your meal! First, you will want to place your cooked pasta back into the pot. Once in place, you can add in your vegetables and sauce. You will want to give everything a good stir so you can coat everything with the sauce, evenly. With everything in place, turn the heat to low and cook everything until it is warm. If needed, feel free to add in water to keep your meal from drying out. Serve warm and enjoy!

Nutrition Values:

Calories: 230

Protein: 14g

Fat: 9g

Carbs: 32g

Fibers: 5g

Quinoa Salad

Time: Twenty-five Minutes

Servings: Four

Ingredients:

- Sunflower Seeds (.50 C.)
- Sun Died Tomatoes (.25 C.)
- Parsley (.25 C.)
- Fresh Dill (.25 C.)
- Lemon (1)
- Chickpeas (1 Can)
- Broccoli Florets (3 C.)
- Red Onion (.25 C.)
- Olive Oil (2 T.)
- Dry Quinoa (1 C.)

Directions:

1. To start this recipe, you will first want to cook your quinoa according to the directions included on the package.

2. Once the quinoa is cooked through, you can bring a skillet over medium heat. Once the pan is warm, pour in the olive oil and bring the oil to a gentle sizzle. At this point, you will now add in the broccoli and red onion. When the vegetables are in place, cook them for five minutes or until they are both soft.

3. Next, you will want to take a large salad bowl and place your quinoa, dill, parsley, sun-dried tomatoes, chickpeas, red onion, and the cooked broccoli.

4. For extra flavor, squeeze the juice of one lemon over everything in the bowl. Once this is done, give the salad a toss, season with salt and pepper, and enjoy your meal!

Nutrition Values:

Calories: 460

Protein: 17g

Fat: 19g

Carbs: 62g

Fibers: 13g

Green Curry Tofu

Time: One Hour

Servings: Four

Ingredients:

- Lime Juice (1 T.)
- Tamari Sauce (1 T.)
- Water Chestnuts (8 Oz.)
- Green Beans (1 C.)
- Salt (.50 t.)
- Vegetable Broth (.50 C.)
- Coconut Milk (14 Oz.)
- Chickpeas (1 C.)
- Green Curry Paste (3 T.)
- Frozen Edamame (1 C.)
- Garlic Cloves (2)
- Ginger (1 inch)
- Olive Oil (1 t.)
- Diced Onion (1)
- Extra-firm Tofu (8 Oz.)
- Brown Basmati Rice (1 C.)

Directions:

1. To start, you will want to cook your rice according to the directions on the package. You can do this in a rice cooker or simply on top of the stove.

2. Next, you will want to prepare your tofu. You can remove the tofu from the package and set it on a plate. Once in place, set another plate on top and something heavy so you can begin to drain the tofu. Once the tofu is prepared, cut it into half inch cubes.

3. Next, take a medium-sized pan and place it over medium heat. As the pan heats up, go ahead and place your olive oil. When the olive oil begins to sizzle, add your onions and cook until they turn a nice translucent color. Typically, this process will take about five minutes. When your onions are ready, add in the garlic and ginger. With these in place, cook the ingredients for another two to three minutes.

4. Once the last step is done, add in your curry paste and edamame. Cook these two ingredients until the edamame is no longer frozen.

5. With these ready, you will now add in the cubed tofu, chickpeas, vegetable broth, coconut milk, and the salt. When everything is in place, you will want to bring the pot to a simmer. Add in the water chestnuts and green beans next and cook for a total of five minutes.

6. When all of the ingredients are cooked through, you can remove the pan from the heat and divide your meal into bowls. For extra flavor, try stirring in tamari, lime juice, or soy sauce. This recipe is excellent served over rice or any other side dish!

Nutrition Values:

Calories: 760

Protein: 23g

Fat: 38g

Carbs: 89g

Fibers: 9g

African Peanut Protein Stew

Time: Forty-five Minutes

Servings: Four

Ingredients:

- Basmati Rice (1 Package)
- Roasted Peanuts (.25 C.)
- Baby Spinach (2 C.)
- Chickpeas (15 Oz.)
- Chili Powder (1.50 t.)
- Vegetable Broth (4 C.)
- Natural Peanut Butter (.33 C.)
- Pepper (.25 t.)
- Salt (.25 t.)
- Diced Tomatoes (28 Oz.)
- Chopped Sweet Potato (1)
- Diced Jalapeno (1)
- Diced Red Pepper (1)
- Sweet Onion (1)
- Olive Oil (1 t.)

Directions:

1. First, you will want to cook your onion. You will do this by heating olive oil in a large saucepan over medium heat. Once the olive oil is sizzling, add in the onion and cook for five minutes or so. The onion will turn translucent when it is cooked through.

2. With the onion done, you will now add in the canned tomatoes, diced sweet potato, jalapeno, and bell peppers. Simmer all of these ingredients over a medium to high heat for about five minutes. If desired, you can season these vegetables with salt and pepper.

3. As the vegetables cook, you will want to make your sauce. You will do this by taking a bowl and mix together one cup of vegetable broth with the peanut butter. Be sure to mix well, so there are no clumps. Once this is done, pour the sauce into the saucepan along with three more cups of vegetable broth. At this point, you will want to season the dish with cayenne and chili powder.

4. Next, cover your pan and reduce to a lower heat. Go ahead and allow these ingredients to simmer for about ten to twenty minutes. At the end of this time, the sweet potato should be nice and tender.

5. Last, you will want to add in the spinach and chickpeas. Give everything a good stir to mix together. You will want to cook this dish until the spinach begins to wilt. Once again, you can add salt and pepper as needed.

6. Finally, serve your dish over rice, garnish with peanuts, and enjoy!

Nutrition Values:

Calories: 440

Protein: 16g

Fat: 13g

Carbs: 69g

Fibers: 12g

Thai Zucchini Noodle Salad

Time: Twenty-five Minutes

Servings: Four

Ingredients:

- Peanuts (.50 C.)
- Peanut Sauce (.50 C.)
- Water (2 T.)
- Extra-firm Tofu (.50 Block)
- Chopped Green Onions (.25 C.)
- Spiralized Carrot (1)
- Spiralized Zucchini (3)

Directions:

1. First, you are going to want to create your peanut sauce. To do this, take a small bowl and slowly mix your peanut sauce with water. You will want to add one tablespoon at a time to achieve the thickness you desire.

2. Next, you will combine all of the ingredients from above, minus the peanuts, into a large mixing bowl. Once everything is in place, top with the salad dressing and give everything a good toss to assure even coating.

3. Finally, sprinkle your peanuts on top, and your meal is done!

Nutrition Values:
Calories: 200
Protein: 13g
Fat: 13g
Carbs: 11g
Fibers: 5g

Spicy Chickpea Sandwich

Time: Twenty Minutes

Servings: Four

Ingredients:

- Raisins (.25 C.)
- Spinach Leaves (.50 C.)
- Red Onion (.50)
- Red Pepper (.50)
- Ground Cumin (.50 t.)
- Turmeric (.25 t.)
- Garam Masala Powder (1 T.)
- Olive Oil (2 T.)
- Garlic (1)
- Chickpeas (14 Oz.)
- Fresh Coriander (4 T.)
- Salt (.25 t.)
- Bread (8 Slices)

Directions:

1. To start, you will want to get out your blender. When you are set, add in the chickpeas, olive oil, juice of one lemon, and garlic clove. Blend everything together until the ingredients create a chunky paste.

2. With the chickpea paste made, transfer it into a bowl and mix in the cumin powder, turmeric, and the curry

powder. Give everything a good stir to make sure there are no chunks in your chickpea paste.

3. Next, add in chopped onion and red pepper into the paste. At this point, you can also add in the chopped coriander and raisins. If you would like, feel free to season with salt and lemon juice at this point as well.

4. Finally, take your bread, spread the chickpea mix, top with some spinach leaves, and enjoy a nice protein packed sandwich!

Nutrition Values:

Calories: 280

Protein: 8g

Fat: 8g

Carbs: 48g

Fibers: 8g

Split Pea and Cauliflower Stew

Time: One Hour

Servings: Four

Ingredients:

- Green Onions (.25 C.)
- Chopped Cilantro (.25 C.)
- Salt (1.50 t.)
- Garam Masala (1 t.)
- Apple Cider Vinegar (2 t.)
- Light Coconut Milk (15 Oz.)
- Vegetable Broth (2 C.)
- Ground Turmeric (1 t.)
- Curry Powder (3 t.)
- Minced Garlic (6)
- Chopped Carrots (2)
- Chopped Onion (1)
- Cumin Seeds (1 t.)
- Mustard Seeds (1 t.)
- Spinach Leaves (3 C.)
- Chopped Cauliflower (1)
- Cooked Split Peas (2 C.)

Directions:

1. Before you begin cooking this recipe, you will want to prepare your split peas according to the directions on their package.

2. Once your split peas are cooked, you will want to preheat your oven to 375 degrees. Once warm, place your chopped cauliflower pieces onto a baking sheet and pop it into the oven for ten to fifteen minutes. By the end, the cauliflower should be tender and slightly brown.

3. Next, you will want to place a large pot on your stove and turn the heat to medium. As the pot heats up, add in the oil, cumin seeds, and mustard seeds. Within sixty seconds, the seeds will begin popping. You will want to make sure you are stirring these ingredients frequently, so they do not burn.

4. Now that the seeds and oil are warm, you can add in your onion, garlic, ginger, and chopped carrots. Cook these for five minutes or until the carrot and onion are nice and soft. Once they are, you can add in your turmeric and curry powder. Be sure to gently mix everything together so you can evenly coat the vegetables.

5. After one minute of allowing the vegetables to soak up the spices, you will want to add in the coconut milk, split peas, and vegetable broth. At this point, you will want to lower the heat to low and place a cover over your pot. Allow all of the ingredients to simmer for about twenty minutes. As everything cooks, be sure to stir the pot occasionally to make sure nothing sticks to the bottom.

6. Finally, you will want to stir in the garam masala, apple cider vinegar, and the roasted cauliflower. If needed, you can also add salt as desired. When these ingredients are in place, go ahead and allow the stew to simmer for another ten minutes or so.

7. As a final touch, feel free to top your stew with green onions and chopped cilantro for extra flavors!

Nutrition Values:

Calories: 700

Protein: 31g

Fat: 31g

Carbs: 84g

Fibers: 34g

Black Bean and Pumpkin Chili

Time: One Hour

Servings: Four

Ingredients:

- Garbanzo Beans (1 Can)
- Black Beans (1 Can)
- Vegetable Stock (1 C.)
- Tomatoes (1 C.)
- Pumpkin Puree (1 C.)
- Chopped Onion (1)
- Olive Oil (1 T.)
- Chili Powder (2 T.)
- Cumin Powder (1 T.)
- Salt (.25 t.)
- Pepper (.25 t.)

Directions:

1. To begin, you will want to place a large pot over medium heat. At the pot warms up, place your olive oil, garlic, and chopped onion into the bottom. Allow this mixture to cook for about five minutes or until the onion is soft.

2. At this point, you will now want to add in the garbanzo beans, black beans, vegetable stock, canned tomatoes, and pumpkin. If you do not have any vegetable stock on hand, you can also use water.

3. With your ingredients in place, add in the half of the chili powder, half of the cumin, and any salt and pepper according to your own taste. Once the spices are in place, give the chili a quick taste and add more as needed.
4. Now, bring the pot to a boil and stir all of the ingredients together to assure the spices are spread evenly throughout your dish.
5. Last, bring the pot to a simmer and cook everything for about twenty minutes. When the twenty minutes are done, remove the pot from the heat, and enjoy!

Nutrition Values:

Calories: 390

Protein: 19g

Fat: 8g

Carbs: 65g

Fibers: 21g

Matcha Tofu Soup

Time: One Hour

Servings: Four

Ingredients:

- Vegetable Broth (.50 C.)
- Extra-firm Tofu (1 Package)
- Light Coconut Milk (13.5 Oz.)
- Kale (5 C.)
- Garlic Powder (.25 t.)
- Smoked Paprika (.25 t)
- Ground Black Pepper (.25 t.)
- Mirin (1 t.)
- Soy Sauce (2 T.)
- Cilantro (1 C.)
- Matcha Powder (2 t.)
- Vegetable Broth (4 C.)
- Ground Black Pepper (.25 t.)
- Cayenne Pepper (.25 t.)
- Garlic (1 t.)
- Minced Garlic (3)
- Chopped Potato (1)
- Chopped Onion (1)

Directions:

1. To start, you will want to place a large pot over medium heat. As the pot warms up, add a splash of vegetable broth to the bottom and begin to cook the chopped potato and onion. Typically, it will take eight to ten minutes until they are nice and soft. When the vegetables are ready, you can then add in the black pepper, cayenne pepper, ginger, and garlic. Sauté these ingredients for another minute.

2. When these vegetables are prepared, you can add in the kale and cook for a few more minutes. Once the kale begins to wilt, stir in the rest of the vegetable broth and bring your soup to a boil. Once boiling, reduce the heat, cover the pot, and simmer all of the ingredients for thirty minutes. After fifteen minutes, remove the top so you can stir in the matcha and cilantro.

3. Once the thirty minutes are done, remove the pot from the heat and allow the soup to cool for a little. Once cool, place the mixture into a blender and gently stir in the coconut milk. Blend the soup on high until you reach a silky and smooth consistency for the soup.

4. Finally, cook your tofu according to your own preference. Be sure to chop the tofu into cubes and brown on all sides. Once cooked, place the tofu in your soup and enjoy!

Nutrition Values:

Calories: 450

Protein: 20g

Fat: 32g

Carbs: 27g

Fibers: 7g

Sweet Potato Tomato Soup

Time: One Hour

Servings: Four

Ingredients:

- Water or Vegetable Stock (1 L.)
- Tomato Puree (2 T.)
- Garlic (3)
- Chopped Onion (1)
- Red Lentils (1 C.)
- Chopped Carrots (3)
- Chopped Sweet Potato (1)
- Salt (.25 t.)
- Pepper (.25 t.)
- Ginger (.50 t.)
- Chili Powder (.50 t.)

Directions:

1. First, we are going to prepare the vegetables for this recipe. You will do this by preheating your oven to 350 degrees. While the oven heats up, you will want to peel and cut both your sweet potato and the carrots. Once they are prepared, place them on a baking sheet and drizzle them with olive oil. You can also add salt and pepper if you would like. When you are ready, place the sheet into the oven for forty minutes. By the end, the vegetables should be nice and soft.

2. As the sweet potato and carrots get baked in the oven, place a medium-sized pan over medium heat and begin to cook your garlic and onion. After five minutes or so, you will want to add in your cooked lentils, tomato, and the spices from the list above. By the end, the lentils should be soft.
3. Finally, you will add all of the ingredients into a blender and blend until the soup if perfectly smooth.

Nutrition Values:

Calories: 350

Protein: 16g

Fat: 11g

Carbs: 48g

Fibers: 19g

Baked Spicy Tofu Sandwich

Time: Forty-five Minutes

Servings: Four

Ingredients:

- Whole Grain Bread (8)
- Maple Syrup (1 T.)
- White Miso Paste (1 T.)
- Tomato Paste (1 T.)
- Liquid Smoke (1 Dash)
- Soy Sauce (1 T.)
- Cumin (1 t.)
- Paprika (.50 t.)
- Chipotles in Adobo Sauce (1 t.)
- Vegetable Broth (1 C.)
- Tofu (16 Oz.)
- Tomato (1)
- Chopped Red Onion (.25 C.)
- Tabasco (1 Dash)
- Lime (1)
- Cumin (.25 t.)
- Chili Powder (.25 t.)
- Coriander (.25 t.)
- Cilantro (.25 C.)
- Avocado (1)

- Ground Black Pepper (.25 t.)
- Garlic (2)
- Lime (.50)

Directions:

1. To prepare for this recipe, you will want to prep your tofu the night before. To start, you will want to press the tofu for a few hours. Once this is done, cut the tofu into eight slices and then place them in the freezer.

2. When you are ready, it is time to make the marinade for the tofu. To do this, take a bowl and mix together the vegetable broth, tomato paste, maple syrup, and all of the spices from the list above. Be sure to stir everything together to get the spices spread through the vegetable broth. Once it is mixed together, add in your thawed slices of tofu and soak them for a few hours.

3. Once the tofu is marinated, heat your oven to 425 degrees. When the oven is warm, place the tofu on a baking sheet and place in the oven for twenty minutes. At the end of this time, the tofu should be nice and crispy on the top and edges.

4. When your tofu is cooked to your liking, layer it on your bread slices with your favorite toppings. This sandwich can be enjoyed cold or warm!

Nutrition Values:
Calories: 390
Protein: 21g
Fat: 16g
Carbs: 49g
Fibers: 11g

Vegetable Stir-Fry

Time: Forty-five Minutes

Servings: Three

Ingredients:

- Zucchini (.50)
- Red Bell Pepper (.50)
- Broccoli (.50)
- Red Cabbage (1 C.)
- Brown Rice (.50 C.)
- Tamari Sauce (2 T.)
- Red Chili Pepper (1)
- Fresh Parsley (.25 t.)
- Garlic (4)
- Olive Oil (2 T.)
- Optional: Sesame Seeds

Directions:

1. To begin, you will want to cook your brown rice according to the directions that are placed on the package. Once this step is done, place the brown rice in a bowl and put it to the side.

2. Next, you will want to take a frying pan and place some water in the bottom. Bring the pan over medium heat and then add in your chopped vegetables. Once in place, cook the vegetables for five minutes or until they are tender.

3. When the vegetables are cooked through, you will then want to add in the parsley, cayenne powder, and the garlic. You will want to cook this mixture for a minute or so. Be sure you stir the ingredients so that nothing sticks to the bottom of your pan.

4. Now, add in the rice and tamari to your pan. You will cook this mixture for a few more minutes or until everything is warmed through.

5. For extra flavor, try adding sesame seeds before you enjoy your lunch! If you have any left-overs, you can keep this stir-fry in a sealed container for about five days in your fridge.

Nutrition Values:

Calories: 280

Protein: 10g

Fat: 12g

Carbs: 38g

Fibers: 6g

Kale Protein Bowl

Time: Thirty Minutes

Servings: Two

Ingredients:

- Water (.75 C.)
- Maple Syrup (1 t.)
- Turmeric (2 t.)
- Ground Ginger (.50 t.)
- Ground Ginger (.50 t.)
- Coconut Aminos (2 T.)
- Lime Juice (2 T.)
- Tahini (.50 C.)
- Hemp Seeds (.25 C.)
- Tempeh (4 Oz.)
- Broccoli (2 C.)
- Kale (3 C.)
- Minced Garlic (1)
- Coconut Oil (1 T.)
- Quinoa (1 C.)

Directions:

1. Before you put together your bowl, you will want to make your quinoa. Place your quinoa with two cups of water into a pot. Once in place, bring the pot to a boil

and reduce the heat. Allow the quinoa to simmer for fifteen minutes or until all of the water in the pot is gone. In the end, the quinoa will be nice and fluffy.

2. Once your quinoa is cooked, take a small saucepan and begin to melt the coconut oil. When the oil begins to sizzle, place your red onion, tempeh, broccoli, kale, and garlic. Cook everything together for about five minutes. By the end, the vegetables should be cooked through and tender.

3. Now, portion the quinoa into two to three bowls. Once in place, you can top the quinoa off with your cooked vegetables. For extra flavor, drizzle tahini over the top and sprinkle raw hemp seeds. Enjoy!

Nutrition Values:

Calories: 920

Protein: 38g

Fat: 48g

Carbs: 95g

Fibers: 16g

Chapter Four: Dinner Recipes

Veggie Pad Thai

Time: Thirty Minutes

Servings: Four

Ingredients:

- Sesame Seeds (1 T.)
- Peanuts (.50 C.)
- Sesame Oil (2 t.)
- Lime Juice (2 T.)
- Rice Vinegar (2 T.)
- Tomato Paste (1 T.)
- Soy Sauce (.25 C.)
- Brown Sugar (.25 C.)
- Chopped Green Onions (4)
- Minced Garlic Cloves (1)
- Red Pepper (.50)
- Spiralized Zucchini (2)
- Chopped Broccoli (1)
- Rice Noodles (1 C.)
- Chopped Extra-Firm Tofu (.50)
- Olive Oil (2 T.)
- Cilantro (.25 C.)
- Optional: Parsley

Directions:

1. To start, you are going to want to heat up a large pan over medium heat. Once the pan is warm, go ahead and place a tablespoon of the olive oil. As the oil begins to sizzle, carefully place your tofu and cook until it is browned on all sides. Typically, this will take between five and ten minutes. When the tofu is cooked to your liking, remove it from the pan and place it to the side.

2. Next, you will want to bring a pot of water over high heat. Allow the water to boil and then add in your rice noodles. At this time, you will want to cook the noodles according to the directions provided on the side of the package.

3. As the rice noodles are cooking, you can continue cooking in your large pan. Now, you will want to place another tablespoon of olive oil and allow it to sizzle. Once it is warm, add in the red pepper, zucchini, and broccoli. You will cook these vegetables for five to ten minutes. You will cook these through until they are soft and tender. Once the vegetables are soft, add in the garlic and cook for another two minutes.

4. Once the rice noodles are cooked, drain the water and then place them in the same pan as the vegetables. After you have given these ingredients a good stir, add in the tofu and then toss everything together.

5. Now, lower your temperature and allow the vegetables to cook a bit longer. As they cook, take a small bowl and begin to make your sauce. All you need to do is combine the soy sauce, brown sugar, tomato paste, rice vinegar, garlic powder, sesame oil, and the lime juice. Once combined, carefully pour it over the ingredients in your pan.

6. Finally, divide your meal into bowls. For extra flavor, try adding chopped cilantro, parsley, sesame seeds, and even peanuts!

Nutrition Values:

Calories: 620

Protein: 23g

Fat: 27g

Carbs: 79g

Fibers: 12g

Vegan Cheesy Mac and Cheese

Time: Thirty Minutes

Servings: Eight

Ingredients:

- Tahini (1 T.)
- Turmeric (.50 t.)
- Paprika (.50 t.)
- Dry Mustard (.50 t.)
- Garlic Puree (.50 t.)
- Salt (1 t.)
- Lemon Juice (1 T.)
- Corn Starch (3 T.)
- Nutritional Yeast (.75 C.)
- Almond Milk (1 C.)
- Water (1.25 C.)
- Pasta (1 Lb.)
- Black Pepper (.25 t.)

Directions:

1. To start off, you will want to prepare your pasta according to the directions that are provided on the side of the box.

2. As the pasta is cooking, you will want to include the rest of the ingredients from the list above into a blender and

blend until smooth. Typically, this will take thirty to sixty seconds.

3. When your pasta is ready, place it in a pot and pour the sauce of the top. Once everything is in place, go ahead and turn the heat to low or medium. As the pot begins to warm up, stir everything together frequently. It will take the sauce anywhere from five to ten minutes to thicken properly. If you are looking to get more vegetables into your day, feel free to add red bell pepper, spinach, or any of your favorite vegetables for some extra flavor.

Nutrition Values:

Calories: 310

Protein: 16g

Fat: 4g

Carbs: 55g

Fibers: 7g

Sweet Potato Gnocchi

Time: One Hour

Servings: Four

Ingredients:

- Flour (2 C.)
- Salt (.25 t.)
- Turmeric (.50 t.)
- Roasted Garlic (3)
- Sweet Potato (1)

Directions:

1. To begin this recipe, you will want to heat your oven to 375 degrees. Once the oven is warm, place the sweet potato on a baking sheet and pop it in for thirty minutes. During the last five minutes of the bake time, add the garlic cloves into the oven and allow them to roast. When the time is up, remove the baking sheet from the oven and allow the ingredients to cool for ten minutes or so.

2. Next, you will want to remove the skin of the sweet potato. Once this is done, place the sweet potato into a mixing bowl and add in the garlic. Carefully take a fork and mash everything together until there are no chunks. At this point, you can season the sweet potato with the turmeric and salt.

3. With the sweet potato now seasoned, it is time to add the flour. You will want to add the flour in a half of a cup at a time. Be sure to stir the ingredients together well before you add any more flour in. The amount of flour

may vary depending on the size of the sweet potato. You will want to continue adding flour until it becomes difficult to stir.

4. Now, your sweet potato should have a dough-like consistency. Break the dough up and roll the sweet potato into strips. Using a knife, you can cut these strips into half-inch pieces.

5. Once you have finished making your gnocchi, you will want to take a large pot of water and bring it to a boil over high heat. Once the water is boiling, carefully drop in the gnocchi pieces. When they are cooked through, the pieces will rise to the top. Typically, this will take two to three minutes. Enjoy!

Nutrition Values:

Calories: 260

Protein: 10g

Fat: 1g

Carbs: 55g

Fibers: 3g

Taco Pasta Bowl

Time: Thirty Minutes

Servings: Four

Ingredients:

- Black Beans (1 Can)
- Corn (1 C.)
- Diced Onion (.50 C.)
- Salsa (1 Jar)
- Pasta (1 Box)
- Cumin (.25 t.)
- Chili Powder (2 T.)

Directions:

1. To start, please cook the pasta of your choice according to the directions provided on the box. Once this step is complete, you can drain the water and set the pasta to the side.

2. Next, you will want to take a medium pan and place it over medium to high heat. Add one tablespoon of your oil and bring it to sizzle. Once the oil is hot, place your onion and cook for three to five minutes. By the end, the onion should be soft.

3. At this point, you will add in the beans, corn, salsa, and spices. I have chosen to use chili powder and cumin, but you can spice your dish however you would like!

4. Last, you will pour your sauce over your pasta and enjoy!

Nutrition Values:

Calories: 530

Protein: 22g

Fat: 3g

Carbs: 107g

Fibers: 14g

Avocado Pasta

Time: Twenty Minutes

Servings: Four

Ingredients:

- Corn (.50 C.)
- Cherry Tomatoes (1 C.)
- Olive Oil (.33 C.)
- Black Pepper (.25 t.)
- Salt (.25 t.)
- Lemon Juice (2 T.)
- Garlic Cloves (2)
- Basil Leaves (.50 C.)
- Avocados (2)
- Spaghetti (12 Oz.)

Directions:

1. To begin this easy recipe, you will first want to cook your pasta. You will want to do this step according to the directions provided on the pasta's package. Once the pasta is cooked through, drain the water and place the pasta to the side.

2. As the pasta is cooking, you can begin to make your avocado sauce. To do this, you will be placing the lemon juice, garlic, basil, and pitted avocados into a food processor. When everything is in place, go ahead and season the ingredients with salt and pepper according to your own taste. As you run the processor, carefully add

the olive oil until you achieve a creamy texture for your sauce.

3. Now, take a large bowl and place your pasta. Gently pour the sauce over the top and stir everything together. As a final touch, add in the corn and cherry tomatoes. Serve immediately and enjoy your dinner!

Nutrition Values:

Calories: 670

Protein: 18g

Fat: 35g

Carbs: 78g

Fibers: 10g

Broccoli Over Orzo

Time: Twenty-five Minutes

Servings: Three

Ingredients:

- Olive Oil (3 t.)
- Smashed Garlic Cloves (4)
- Broccoli Florets (2 C.)
- Orzo Pasta (4.50 Oz.)
- Salt (.25 t.)
- Pepper (.25 t.)

Directions:

1. Start off by preparing your broccoli. You can do this by trimming the stems off and slicing the broccoli into small, bite-size pieces. If you want, go ahead and season with salt.

2. Next, you will want to steam your broccoli over a little bit of water until it is cooked through. Once the broccoli is cooked, chop it up into even smaller pieces.

3. When the broccoli is done, cook your pasta according to the directions provided on the box. Once this is done, drain the water and then place the pasta back into the pot.

4. With the pasta and broccoli done, place it back into the pot with the garlic. Stir everything together well and cook until the garlic turns a nice golden color. Be sure to stir everything to combine your meal well. Serve warm and enjoy a simple dinner!

Nutrition Values:

Calories: 230

Protein: 10g

Fat: 5g

Carbs: 39g

Fibers: 5g

Garlic Zucchini and Lentils

Time: Fifteen Minutes

Servings: Six

Ingredients:

- Zucchini (4)
- Ground Coriander (1 T.)
- Ground Cumin (1 T.)
- Onion (1)
- Cumin Seeds (1 t.)
- Crushed Garlic Cloves (6)
- Olive Oil (2 T.)
- Water (4 C.)
- Salt (2 t.)
- Ground Turmeric (.50 t.)
- Lentils (1 C.)
- Coriander (2 T.)
- Paprika (.50 t.)

Directions:

1. To begin, you will want to take a large saucepan and place it over medium heat. As the pan heats up, add in the water, lentils, salt, and turmeric. Bring the ingredients to a boil and then reduce the heat. When you have completed this step, carefully cover the pan and cook the lentils for fifteen to twenty minutes. By the

end, the lentils should be fluffy, and all the liquid will be gone. If the lentils are cooked through, transfer them to a serving bowl and place to the side.

2. Next, you will take another saucepan and place it over medium heat. As the pan warms up, add in the olive oil and garlic. Sauté the garlic for two minutes or until it becomes a nice golden color. At this point, add in the chopped zucchini, onion, and your cumin seeds. Go ahead and cook all of these ingredients for five minutes, or until the zucchini and onion are soft. Finally, add in the cumin and ground coriander. Be sure to stir everything together well to assure even coating of the spices.

3. Last, you are going to divide the lentils into serving bowls and top with the spiced vegetables. For extra flavor, try adding fresh coriander leaves. It is also delicious with a side of warm Indian bread or rice.

Nutrition Values:

Calories: 200

Protein: 10g

Fat: 6g

Carbs: 27g

Fibers: 12g

Vegetable Shepherd's Pie

Time: One Hour

Servings: Six

Ingredients:

- Vegan Butter (4 T.)
- Gold Potatoes (3 Lbs.)
- Mixed Frozen Vegetables (10 Oz.)
- Fresh Thyme (2 t.)
- Vegetable Stock (4 C.)
- Green Lentils (1.50 C.)
- Garlic (2)
- Diced Onion (1)
- Salt (.25 t.)
- Pepper (.25 t.)

Directions:

1. To begin, we will prepare the potatoes. While I enjoy the Gold Potatoes, you can use any of your likings. When you have chosen your potatoes, slice them in half and then bring them to a boil over high heat. Once the potatoes are in place, add some salt and cook for thirty minutes. By the end, the skin should come off fairly easily. When they are done, drain the water and place back into a mixing bowl.

2. When the potatoes are in your mixing bowl, you will want to use a masher to begin breaking the potato apart. If you would like, use some vegan butter to make a

smoother mashed potato. At this point, you will also want to add pepper and salt according to taste. Once this step is complete, place the potatoes to the side.

3. Now, you will want to heat your oven to 425 degrees. As the oven heats up, grease up a baking dish and then set it to the side.

4. Next, you will be taking a large saucepan and placing it over medium heat. Once the pan is warmed up, add in your olive oil, garlic, and onions. Cook these onions until they are caramelized and slightly brown. Typically, this will take about five minutes.

5. When the onions are done, you can add your stock and lentils into the pan. Be sure to give the ingredients a good stir and then add in the salt, pepper, and thyme. As the stock begins to boil, reduce your heat to low and allowing everything to simmer. Now, you will want to cook everything in this pan for about forty minutes. Within the last ten minutes, add in your frozen veggies and allow them to cook through.

6. Once the vegetable mix is cooked through, carefully transfer the ingredients into the baking dish that you prepared a bit earlier. At this point, you can add any extra seasonings you desire. When everything is settled, top the dish with the mashed potatoes and smooth it down with a fork or a spoon.

7. Next, you will place the baking dish on a baking sheet in the case of overflow. When you are ready, pop the dish into the oven for about fifteen minutes. When the dish is cooked through, the mashed potatoes will begin to turn a light brown color. Once you have achieved this, remove the dish from the oven, allow to cool slightly, and enjoy!

Nutrition Values:

Calories: 330

Protein: 20g

Fat: .5g

Carbs: 64g

Fibers: 23g

Vegan BBQ Tofu

Time: One Hour

Servings: Three

Ingredients:

- Vegan BBQ Sauce (.25 C.)
- Pepper (.25 t.)
- Garlic Powder (.25 t.)
- Salt (.25 t.)
- Grapeseed Oil (1 T.)
- Firm Tofu (1 Package)

Directions:

1. Before you begin cooking your tofu, you will want to press it. Generally, this will take thirty to forty-five minutes. If possible, try to press the tofu overnight so that it is ready for you when you need it.

2. Once your tofu is ready, bring a saucepan over medium heat and allow it to warm up. As your saucepan is warming up, slice your tofu into small pieces. Add in a tablespoon of oil and spread your tofu across the pan. At this point, season your tofu and cook for five minutes. Be sure to flip each piece of tofu until it is a nice golden-brown color all over.

3. Finally, remove the tofu from the pan and cover it in BBQ sauce. This meal is excellent alone or with your favorite grain or vegetable.

Nutrition Values:

Calories: 290

Protein: 20g

Fat: 15g

Carbs: 25g

Fibers: 5g

Spicy Kung Pao Tofu

Time: Forty Minutes

Servings: Four

Ingredients:

- Water (1 T.)
- Sesame Oil (1 t.)
- Black Vinegar (2 t.)
- Cornstarch (1 t.)
- Sugar (2 t.)
- Dark Soy Sauce (2 t.)
- Light Soy Sauce (1 T.)
- Scallions (5)
- Sliced Root Ginger (1 In.)
- Minced Garlic (3)
- Sliced Red Pepper (1)
- Sliced Green Pepper (1)
- Cooking Oil (3 T.)
- Extra-firm Tofu (1 Lb.)

Directions:

1. Much like with any tofu you cook, you are going to want to make sure you have pressed all of the liquid out. Please take the time to press your tofu before you begin cooking, this will leave you with the best results. Once drained, you can cut your tofu into small cubes. At this

point, you will also want to cut your green and red pepper into small pieces as well.

2. Next, you will be making the sauce. You can do this by taking a small bowl and mix together the sugar, water, vinegar, cornstarch, garlic, green onion, ginger, salt, and both soy sauces. Be sure to mix everything together well to blend the flavors together.

3. Next, you will want to take a skillet and place it over medium heat. As the pan warms up, add in three tablespoons of your oil and then gently place the tofu cubes. You will cook the tofu until it becomes a nice golden-brown color on all sides. Once your tofu is cooked, add in the peppers and cook them for another five minutes or so. By the end, the pepper will be nice and tender.

4. Finally, you will gently pour in the sauce you made earlier. Be sure to stir the ingredients well, so the tofu becomes well coated. Cook this dish over medium heat for another five minutes or so to allow the sauce to begin to thicken. Mix everything well and serve over noodles or steamed rice.

Nutrition Values:

Calories: 300

Protein: 20g

Fat: 22g

Carbs: 13g

Fibers: 5g

Easy Vegan Tacos

Time: Fifteen Minutes

Servings: Two

Ingredients:

- Taco Shells (8)
- Corn (.25 C.)
- Chopped Cherry Tomatoes (8)
- Chopped Avocado (1)
- Ground Cumin (2 t.)
- Hot Sauce (2 t.)
- Tomato Puree (1 C.)
- Black Beans (2 C.)

Directions:

1. To begin this recipe, you will want to take a pan and place it over medium heat. As the pan begins to warm up, add in the tomato puree, black beans, hot sauce, and cumin. Cook all of these ingredients together for about five minutes or until everything is warmed through. At this point, feel free to season the dish however you would like.

2. Next, you will begin to assemble the tacos. All you need to do is pour in as much or as little bean mixture into each taco. For extra flavor, try topping the tacos with chopped cherry tomatoes, avocado, and even corn! The options are endless when it comes to tacos!

Nutrition Values:

Calories: 330

Protein: 18g

Fat: 33g

Carbs: 89g

Fibers: 19g

Lentil Burgers

Time: Twenty-five Minutes

Servings: Four

Ingredients:

- Bread Crumbs (2 T.)
- Crushed Walnuts (2 T.)
- Soy Sauce (1 t.)
- Cooked Lentils (2 C.)
- Salt (.50 t.)
- Cumin (.25 t.)
- Nutritional Yeast (.25 C.)

Directions:

1. First, you will want to cook your two cups of lentils. You will want to complete this task following the directions provided on the side of the package. Once this step is complete, drain the lentils and place them into a medium-sized bowl. When the lentils are in place, gently mash them until they reach a smooth consistency.

2. At this point, you will want to add in the bread crumbs, crushed walnuts, soy sauce, nutritional yeast, cumin, and the salt. Be sure to mix everything together and then begin to form your patties. They should be about four inches in diameter and only an inch thick.

3. With your patties formed, you will want to heat a medium size pan over medium heat and begin to warm it. Once warm, add in oil and cook each patty for two to

three minutes on each side. By the end, each side of the burger should be crisp and brown.

4. Finally, serve on a warm bun with your favorite vegan condiments and garnish!

Nutrition Values:

Calories: 410

Protein: 31g

Fat: 5g

Carbs: 65g

Fibers: 33g

Black Bean Meatloaf

Time: One Hour

Servings: Four

Ingredients:

- Chopped Red Bell Pepper (1)
- Quick Oats (1.50 C.)
- Black Beans (2 Cans)
- Ketchup (3 T.)
- Cumin (1 t.)
- Liquid Aminos (1 T.)
- Minced Garlic (1)
- Minced Onion (1)
- Chopped Carrot (1)
- Black Pepper (.25 t.)

Directions:

1. First, you will want to heat your oven to 350 degrees. While the oven warms up, you can begin preparing your dinner.

2. Over medium heat, place a medium sized pan and begin to sauté your onions. You can use water or oil to complete this step. As the onion turns translucent, add in your carrot pieces, pepper, and the garlic. You will want to cook these ingredients for six to eight minutes. By the end, the carrots and pepper should be nice and soft.

3. Next, you will want to get out a large bowl. In this bowl, carefully combine the oats, black beans, and all of the seasonings from the list above. Once these are in place, add in the vegetables you just cooked and mash everything together. Combine all of the ingredients well but not enough to make the mixture mushy. If the ingredients are too hard to form a "dough," add water or moist oats to help hold everything together.

4. When your dough is ready, you can pour it into a lined loaf pan. Once in place, pop the dish into your heated oven for about thirty minutes. By the end, the edges should develop a nice, browned crust. At this point, you will want to remove the dish from the oven and allow it to cool for a bit.

5. This meal is fantastic alone or can be served with your favorite vegetable side!

Nutrition Values:

Calories: 360

Protein: 18g

Fat: 3g

Carbs: 68g

Fibers: 20g

Easy Noodle Alfredo

Time: Thirty Minutes

Servings: Four

Ingredients:

- Green Peas (1 C.)
- Vegan Parmesan Cheese (.25 C.)
- Garlic Powder (.50 t.)
- Nutritional Yeast (6 T.)
- Pepper (.25 t.)
- Salt (.25 t.)
- Unsweetened Almond Milk (2 C.)
- All Purpose Flour (2 T.)
- Minced Garlic (4)
- Olive Oil (3 T.)
- Linguini (10 Oz.)

Directions:

1. First things first—you will want to cook your linguini. Once this step is complete, drain the water and set the cooked pasta to the side for now.

2. Next, you will take a large skillet and place it over medium heat. As the pan warms up, carefully add in your garlic and olive oil. You will want to stir these to assure nothing burns to the bottom of your pan.

3. When you begin to smell the garlic, turn the heat down a tad. Once this is done, add in the flour and cook for about a minute in the olive oil alone. Next, you will add

in the almond milk a little bit at a time. Be sure to whisk the ingredients together to help avoid forming clumps in your sauce. Go ahead and cook this sauce for another two minutes or so.

4. Once your sauce is done, remove from the heat and allow it to cool for a minute or so. When it is safe to handle, transfer the liquid into a blender. When it is in place, add in the garlic, nutritional yeast, vegan parmesan cheese, pepper, and salt according to your taste. Go ahead and blend the mixture on high until you create a nice smooth and creamy sauce. Feel free to adjust your seasonings as you go.

5. Next, you will want to return the sauce to your pan and place it over medium heat until it begins to bubble. Once the bubbles form, turn the heat to low and allow the sauce to thicken. Remember to stir your dish frequently to avoid it burning to the bottom.

6. As you stir the sauce, add more milk if it is too thick. If the sauce is too thin, remove some liquid and add in some extra flour. When the sauce is ready, add it to your pasta and top with cooked peas. For extra flavor, try serving your meal with extra parmesan cheese or even red pepper flakes.

Nutrition Values:

Calories: 470

Protein: 23g

Fat: 7g

Carbs: 82g

Fibers: 10g

Hot Potato Curry

Time: One Hour

Servings: Six

Ingredients:

- Coconut Milk (14 Oz.)
- Peas (15 Oz)
- Garbanzo Beans (15 Oz.)
- Diced Tomatoes (14.5 Oz.)
- Salt (2 t.)
- Minced Ginger Root (1)
- Garam Masala (4 t.)
- Curry Powder (4 t.)
- Cayenne Pepper (1.50 t.)
- Ground Cumin (2 t.)
- Minced Garlic (3)
- Diced Yellow Onion (1)
- Vegetable Oil (2 T.)
- Cubed Potatoes (4)

Directions:

1. To start, you will want to cook your potatoes. All you need to do is bring a pot of water over high heat until the water begins to boil. When the water begins to boil, reduce the heat and place a cover over the pot. Simmer

the potatoes in the water for about fifteen minutes and then drain the water.

2. As the potatoes are cooking, you will want to bring a large skillet over medium heat. As the pan begins to warm up, place your vegetable oil and onion. Cook the onion for five minutes or until it becomes soft. Now, add in the salt, ginger, garam masala, curry powder, cayenne pepper, cumin, and the garlic. At this point, you will want to cook all of these ingredients for two or three minutes.

3. Once the ingredients are warmed through, add in the cooked potatoes, peas, tomatoes, and the garbanzo beans. When these are all in place, carefully pour in the coconut milk and allow the pan to come to a simmer. Simmer this dish for five to ten minutes and then remove from heat.

4. This dish is delicious by itself, but feel free to serve with any of your favorite side dishes!

Nutrition Values:

Calories: 640

Protein: 23g

Fat: 25g

Carbs: 87g

Fibers: 22g

Spinach and Red Lentil Masala

Time: Forty-five Minutes

Servings: Four

Ingredients:

- Baby Spinach (2 C.)
- Red Lentils (1 C.)
- Coconut Milk (15 Oz.)
- Salt (1 t.)
- Diced Tomatoes (15 Oz.)
- Coriander (.25 t.)
- Garam Masala (1 t.)
- Ground Cumin (1 t.)
- Chili Pepper (1)
- Minced Ginger (1 In.)
- Minced Garlic (2)
- Diced Red Onion (1)
- Olive Oil (1 T.)

Directions:

1. To begin, place a large pot over a medium to high heat. As the pot warms up, you can add in your tablespoon of olive oil and the onion. Cook the onion for five minutes or until it becomes soft. Once it does, you can add in the coriander, garam masala, cumin, chili pepper, ginger,

and the garlic. When everything is in place, cook the ingredients for an extra two to three minutes.

2. Once the ingredients from the step above are warmed through, you will want to carefully add the tomatoes and season everything with salt according to your taste. If there are any brown bits on the bottom of the pan, be sure to scrape them up and keep stirring everything. As you continue to cook, the liquid should reduce in about five minutes.

3. Next, pour in the coconut milk along with one cup of water. Once in place, turn the heat up to high and bring the pot to a boil. At this point, you can add in the lentils and reduce the heat back to medium or so. Now, cook the lentils for twenty-five to thirty-five minutes. By the end, the lentils should be nice and tender!

4. Finally, fold in your spinach and cook for an additional five minutes. Once the spinach has wilted, remove the pot from the heat and allow to cool slightly. You can serve this delicious meal over coconut rice or enjoy it by itself.

Nutrition Values:

Calories: 490

Protein: 17g

Fat: 30g

Carbs: 44g

Fibers: 20g

Sweet Hawaiian Burger

Time: Forty-five Minutes

Servings: Four

Ingredients:

- Panko Breadcrumbs (1 C.)
- Red Kidney Beans (14 Oz.)
- Vegetable Oil (1 T.)
- Diced Sweet Potato (1.50 C.)
- Minced Garlic (1)
- Soy Sauce (2 T.)
- Apple Cider Vinegar (3 T.)
- Maple Syrup (.50 C.)
- Water (.50 C.)
- Tomato Paste (.50 C.)
- Pineapple Rings (4)
- Salt (.25 t.)
- Pepper (.25 t.)
- Cayenne (.10 t.)
- Ground Cumin (1.50 t.)
- Burger Buns (4)
- Optional: Red Onion, Tomato, Lettuce, Vegan Mayo

Directions:

1. First, you will want to heat your oven to 400 degrees. As the oven warms up, take your sweet potato and toss it in oil. When this step is complete, place the diced sweet potato pieces in a single layer on a baking sheet. Once this is done, pop the sheet into the oven and cook for about twenty minutes. Halfway through, flip the pieces over to assure the sweet potato cooks all the way through. When this is done, remove the sheet from the oven and allow the sweet potato to cool down slightly.

2. Next, you will want to get out your food processor. When you are ready, add in the beans, sweet potatoes, breadcrumbs, cayenne, cumin, soy sauce, garlic, and onion pieces. Once in place, begin to pulse the ingredients together until you have a finely chopped mixture. As you do this, season the "dough" with pepper and salt as desired. Now, shape the dough into four patties.

3. When your patties are formed, begin to heat a large skillet over medium heat. As the pan warms up, place your oil and then grill each side of your patties. Typically, this will take five to six minutes on each side. You will know the burger is cooked through when it is browned on each side.

4. All you need to do now is assemble your burger! If you want, try baking the pineapple rings—three minutes on each side should do the trick! Top your burger with lettuce, tomato, and vegan mayo for some extra flavor.

Nutrition Values:

Calories: 460

Protein: 15g

Fat: 12g

Carbs: 80g

Fibers: 6g

Chapter Five: Snacks and Desserts

Spicy Kale Chips

Time: One Hour

Servings: Four

Ingredients:

- Kale (10 Oz.)
- Garlic Powder (.50 T.)
- Brown Sugar (.50 T.)
- Ancho (2 t.)
- Smoked Paprika (1 T.)
- Chili Powder (.10 t.)
- Nutritional Yeast (.25 C.)
- Minced Garlic (.50 t.)
- Salt (.25 t.)
- Ground Pepper (.50 t.)
- Sriracha (.50 t.)
- Lime Juice (1)
- Garlic Powder (1 t.)
- Sriracha (2 t.)
- Olive Oil (3 T.)

Directions:

1. To make these delicious chips, you will first want to heat your oven to 275 degrees.

2. Next, prepare your kale by removing the stems from the leaves. Once this is done, carefully tear the kale into pieces and then wash them. Carefully dry each piece of kale and place in a large bowl.

3. In a separate bowl, you will want to combine the lime juice, zest from the lime, garlic powder, Sriracha, olive oil, pepper, and salt. Give everything a good stir to assure they are mixed together properly, and all of the flavors have a chance to blend together. Once this step is complete, pour the sauce over the kale and toss to coat.

4. Now, you will want to line a baking sheet with some parchment paper. Once in place, carefully divide the kale in a single layer. When the kale is in place, bake in the oven for thirty-five to forty minutes. Halfway through this time, you will want to rotate your pan to assure even cooking.

5. Finally, remove the pan from the oven, allow to cool, and enjoy your healthy chips!

Nutrition Values:

Calories: 190

Protein: 10g

Fat: 12g

Carbs: 19g

Fibers: 6g

Cinnamon and Maple Quinoa Granola

Time: One Hour

Servings: Two

Ingredients:

- Walnut Oil (2 T.)
- Maple Syrup (.25 C.)
- Salt (.25 t.)
- Cinnamon (2 t.)
- Pumpkin Seeds (.50 C.)
- Chopped Pecans (.50 C.)
- Quinoa (.75 C.)

Directions:

1. To start, heat your oven to 250 degrees. As the oven warms up, you will want to rinse your quinoa and then spread it in a thin layer on a baking tray. Once in place and the oven is warm, bake for fifteen to twenty minutes. By the end, all of the liquid should have evaporated.

2. Once the quinoa is cooked through, remove the baking sheet from the oven. Now, raise the temperature of the oven to 350 degrees. As you wait for the oven to warm up further, take a small bowl so you can combine the oil, maple syrup, salt, cinnamon, pumpkin seeds, and pecans. Be sure to mix everything together well before you spread it into a thin layer on the baking tray. Once in place, pop the baking sheet into the oven for twenty minutes or so.

3. Finally, remove the baking sheet from the oven. Place all of the cooked ingredients into a bowl and stir well. Allow the quinoa and nut mixture to clump together. This recipe makes a fantastic on-the-go snack or served over your favorite vegan foods.

Nutrition Values:

Calories: 650

Protein: 19g

Fat: 33g

Carbs: 73g

Fibers: 8g

Five-Ingredient Protein Bars

Time: Forty Minutes

Servings: Nine

Ingredients:

- Dark Vegan Chocolate (3 T.)
- Peanut Butter (1 C.)
- Maple Syrup (2 T.)
- Vanilla Protein Powder (3 T.)
- Amaranth (.33 C.)

Directions:

1. To begin, you will want to prepare a baking pan by lining it with parchment paper. Once this is done, you can set it to the side.

2. Next, you will want to pop the amaranth. You can do this by taking a large pot and placing it over medium heat. You can tell the amaranth is ready when you drop water into the pot, and it balls up. Carefully add a tablespoon of the amaranth to the pot at a time, place the cover, and shake the pot to help move the grain around. Be sure to pull the amaranth away from the heat after ten seconds to make sure they do not burn. In the end, empty the bowl into a small mixing bowl. It is okay if all of it does not pop!

3. Once your grain is popped, add in the maple syrup and peanut butter. Stir everything together well. Then, add in the vanilla protein powder. When these ingredients are combined well, add in the amaranth and stir to disperse the mixture.

4. Finally, you are going to transfer this mixture to a baking dish. Be sure to press everything down firmly to create an even layer. If you would like, try using a measuring cup to press everything together.
5. When the dough is in place, pop the baking dish into the freezer for ten to fifteen minutes. After this time, the bar should be firm to the touch. At this point, you will want to remove the baking dish from the freezer and cut the ingredients into nine bars.
6. For extra flavor, try melting down some dark chocolate and drizzling it over the top. These bars can be enjoyed at room temperature or stored in the fridge for up to five days.

Nutrition Values:

Calories: 190

Protein: 10g

Fat: 14g

Carbs: 9g

Fibers: 2g

Peanut Butter Power Bites

Time: Fifteen Minutes

Servings: Four

Ingredients:

- Peanut Butter (2 C.)
- Ground Almonds (.33 C.)
- Dehydrated Cranberries (.66 C.)
- Chia Seeds (.10 C.)
- Flax Seeds (.33 C.)
- Rolled Oats (2 C.)
- Grated Carrots (1.50 C.)
- Raw Honey (.50 C.)
- Vanilla Extract (1 t.)

Directions:

1. To start, you are going to take all of the dry ingredients from the list above and mix them in a small mixing bowl. The last ingredient you will want to add in the grated carrots. Once in place, you can use a wooden spoon or your hands to combine everything.

2. Next, you will slowly want to add in the vanilla extract, honey, and the peanut butter. As you mix everything together, you will notice your dough beginning to form. When you feel everything is combined well, pop the bowl into the fridge for about twenty minutes.

3. Once this time has passed, you can remove the bowl and begin rolling bite-sized pieces of your dough. These

snacks can be stored in the fridge or frozen if you plan on keeping them for a while!

Nutrition Values:

Calories: 370

Protein: 10g

Fat: 25g

Carbs: 20g

Fibers: 17g

Black Bean Dip

Time: Twenty Minutes

Servings: Four

Ingredients:

- Chopped Onion (.50)
- Black Beans (30 Oz.)
- Chopped Jalapeno (.50)
- Ground Cumin (.25 t.)
- Chili Powder (.50 t.)
- Salt (.50 t.)
- Lime (.50)
- Minced Garlic (2)

Directions:

1. For this recipe, all you need to do is place all of the ingredients from above into your food processor and mix until smooth! If you would like, feel free to adjust the seasonings as desired.

2. Finally, transfer the dip into the bowl and enjoy with your favorite chips for a quick and healthy snack.

Nutrition Values:

Calories: 210

Protein: 13g

Fat: 0g

Carbs: 40g

Fibers: 16g

Chocolate Chip Protein Cookies

Time: Forty Minutes

Servings: Twelve

Ingredients:

- Agave Nectar (.50 C.)
- Vanilla Extract (1 T.)
- Grapeseed Oil (.50 C.)
- Baking Soda (.50 t.)
- Sea Salt (.50 t.)
- Almond Flour (2.50 C.)
- Vegan Chocolate Chips (.50 C.)

Directions:

1. To begin, you will want to preheat your oven to 350 degrees. As the oven warms up, prepare a baking dish by lining it with parchment paper. Once in place, you can set this to the side.

2. Next, you will take a large bowl and combine all of the dry ingredients together. Once these are in place, carefully add the wet ingredients one at a time. Be sure to stir everything together well to assure it is mixed together completely and there are no dry ingredients.

3. Once your dough has been formed, begin to create half inch balls and spread them evenly on your baking sheet. When there is no dough left, pop the baking sheet into the oven for seven to ten minutes. By the end, your cookies should be golden brown. At this point, you can remove the sheet from the oven, allow the cookies to cool, and enjoy your little treat!

Nutrition Values:

Calories: 210

Protein: 5g

Fat: 19g

Carbs: 7g

Fibers: 3g

Vegan Bean Brownies

Time: One Hour

Servings: Four

Ingredients:

- Walnuts (5)
- Baking Soda (1 t.)
- Vanilla Extract (1 T.)
- Maple Syrup (.50 C.)
- Coconut Oil (4 T.)
- Cocoa Powder (.50 C.)
- Kidney Beans (2 C.)
- Salt (.25 t.)

Directions:

1. First, heat your oven to 325 degrees. As the oven warms up, you can prep your baking dish with parchment paper. When this is all set, you can place it to the side.

2. Next, you will want to place all of the ingredients from the list above into a food processor, minus the walnuts. When everything is in place, carefully blend the ingredients until it creates a dense cream. At this point, you can add in the walnuts and give everything a stir.

3. When you are ready, pour the mixture into the baking dish you prepared a bit earlier. Once in place, pop the whole baking dish into the oven for about thirty minutes. At the end of this time, your brownies should have a nice crust on top. If they are done, remove the brownies from the oven and allow to cool before you enjoy them.

Nutrition Values:

Calories: 250

Protein: 25g

Fat: 19g

Carbs: 90g

Fibers: 18g

Delicious Dessert Pizza

Time: Thirty Minutes

Servings: Eight

Ingredients:

- Fresh Raspberries (12 Oz.)
- Maple Syrup (1 T.)
- Vanilla Extract (.50 t.)
- Coconut Cream (1 C.)
- Maple Syrup (2 T.)
- Coconut Oil (2 T.)
- Cacao Powder (.25 C.)
- Chickpea Flour (.25 C.)
- Vegan Brownie (1 Packet)
- Lemon Zest (1)
- Lemon Juice (1 T.)

Directions:

1. Before you begin cooking this delicious dessert, you are going to want to heat your oven to 350 degrees.

2. As your oven begins to warm up, you will want to get a medium bowl out. Once you have the bowl, combine the cacao powder, chickpea flour, and the vegan brownie mix. Be sure to stir everything together well to assure the ingredients are mixed properly.

3. Next, you will want to take a small bowl and carefully melt your coconut oil. Once it is in liquid form, add in

the maple syrup and then pour this mixture over the dry brownie mixture. Mix everything together until you see a smooth consistency.

4. When your dough has been created, you will want to take your hands and form a big ball with this dough. Place it on a sheet of parchment paper on your counter and roll the ball into a thin circle. You may want to place this on a baking sheet or a small pizza pan. Once it is rolled out, pop the pan into the oven for twelve to fifteen minutes. Once it begins to form a crust, remove from the oven and allow the dough to cool.

5. As the "pizza" is cooking, you will want to take a small pot and place it over medium heat. As the pot warms up, you can add in the lemon juice, lemon zest, and fresh raspberries. At this point, you will want to bring everything to a boil and immediately turn the heat down and allow the raspberries to simmer for ten minutes. Be sure to stir consistently to help break the berries up. By the end, you should have a jam-like consistency. Once finished, remove the pot from the heat and put to the side.

6. Now, you will want to take another small bowl and place your coconut milk. Once in place, carefully beat the coconut milk on high for one or two minutes. As a peak begins to form, add in the vanilla extract and maple syrup. Beat all of these ingredients together until they are well combined.

7. When the brownie is cool, you will want to slice it into eight even pieces. At this point, top the brownie with coconut cream and the raspberry jam you just created. For even more flavor, feel free to add fresh raspberries on top and enjoy!

Nutrition Values:

Calories: 190

Protein: 5g

Fat: 15g

Carbs: 16g

Fibers: 5g

Vanilla and Almond Popsicles

Time: Ten Minutes

Servings: Four

Ingredients:

- Stevia (.50 t.)
- Ground Cinnamon (.75 t.)
- Vanilla Extract (1 t.)
- Almond Butter (.25 C.)
- Nut Milk (1 C.)
- Salt (.25 t.)

Directions:

1. To make these super delicious popsicles, all you have to do is place all of the ingredients from above into a blender, and blend until you achieve a smooth consistency.
2. Once the consistency of desire has been reached, carefully pour the mix into popsicle molds and pop into the freezer for a few hours.
3. When the popsicles are frozen, remove from the freezer and enjoy your tasty treat!

Nutrition Values:

Calories: 100

Protein: 5g

Fat: 9g

Carbs: 4g

Fibers: 1g

Oatmeal and Peanut Butter Cookies

Time: Forty Minutes

Servings: Four

Ingredients:

- Brown Rice Syrup (.33 C.)
- Peanut Butter (.50 C.)
- Mashed Banana (1)
- Coconut (.66 C.)
- Oats (1.25 C.)
- Optional: Vanilla Protein Powder (1 t.)
- Optional: Dried Fruits or Nuts (.25 C.)

Directions:

1. To begin making these delicious cookies, go ahead and heat your oven to 350 degrees. As the oven warms, you can set up a baking sheet with parchment paper and then set it to the side.

2. While the oven is warming up, take a medium-sized bowl and begin to mix together the peanut butter, banana, and the brown rice syrup. You will want to continue stirring this mixture until you reach a smooth consistency. Once achieved, add in the rest of the ingredients in the list above and mix to combine everything.

3. Now that you have your dough, carefully roll half inch balls and place them evenly on your prepared baking sheet. Once in place, press the balls with a fork to form lines within the dough. When this is done, pop the

baking sheet into the oven for twenty-five to thirty minutes. By the end of this time, the cookies should be golden on the edges and nice and soft on the inside.

4. Remove the tray from the oven, allow the cookies to cool for at least ten minutes, and then enjoy!

Nutrition Values:

Calories: 250

Protein: 10g

Fat: 15g

Carbs: 35g

Fibers: 5g

Passion Fruit Mousse

Time: Twenty-five Minutes

Servings: Six

Ingredients:

- Vanilla Protein Powder (2 Scoops)
- Coconut Oil (1 T.)
- Frozen Bananas (2)
- Vanilla Extract (1 t.)
- Coconut Milk (1 Can)
- Passion Fruit Pulp (1 C.)

Directions:

1. First, you will want to take the can of coconut milk and carefully turn it over. At this point, you will want to open the can from the bottom and drain any liquid out. Once this is done, scoop the cream out and place it into a food processor.

2. Once the first step is done, add in the rest of the ingredients from the list above. When everything is in place, blend on high until you achieve a creamy consistency.

3. Place the mixture into the fridge and allow to chill for at least ten minutes before serving.

Nutrition Values:

Calories: 350

Protein: 5g

Fat: 18g

Carbs: 27g

Fibers: 6g

Tiny Strawberry Shortcakes

Time: Forty-five Minutes

Servings: Four

Ingredients:

- Chilled Coconut Cream (1 Can)
- Vanilla Bean Protein Powder (1 Scoop)
- Frozen Strawberries (6)
- Almond Milk (1 C.)
- Melted Coconut Oil (3 T.)
- Maple Syrup (2 T.)
- Coconut Flour (1 C.)
- Sliced Fresh Strawberries (4)

Directions:

1. To start off this recipe, you will first make the shortcake layer. Before you begin, take a muffin tin and line it with papers.

2. Once the tin is prepared, you will want to take a medium-sized bowl and combine the melted coconut oil with the maple syrup and the coconut flour. When these ingredients are placed, slowly begin to add water and stir gently. You will continue to stir until the dough appears crumbly and moldable. At this point, you can press the dough into the bottom of the muffin tins and pop into the freezer.

3. Next, it is time to create the strawberry layer for your strawberry shortcake. To do this, you will want to get

out your food processor or blender. Once in place, add in the almond milk, protein powder, and frozen strawberries. When you are ready, place the blender on high and continue to blend these ingredients until you reach a smooth consistency. Once achieved, carefully spoon the strawberry mixture on top of the shortcake and then place back into the freezer. You will want to keep the cakes in the freezer at least two hours to allow everything to freeze properly.

4. When you are ready to serve, you will want to create the whipped cream last moment. You can do this by taking coconut cream and whipping it for a few minutes. By the end, you should have a light and fluffy whipped cream. When it is ready, spoon a little on each cake and then top with a slice of fresh strawberry. Be sure to allow the cakes to defrost a bit before you enjoy!

Nutrition Values:

Calories: 420

Protein: 8g

Fat: 30g

Carbs: 23g

Fibers: 6g

Chapter Six: Beverage Recipes

Blueberry Breakfast Smoothie

Time: Ten Minutes

Servings: One

Ingredients:

- Coconut Milk Unsweetened (8 Oz.)
- Dates (2)
- Baby Spinach (1 C.)
- Frozen Banana (1)
- Hemp Seeds (.25 C.)
- Avocado (.50)
- Frozen Blueberries (1 C.)
- Optional: Hemp Seeds and Frozen Blueberries

Directions:

1. To create this delicious breakfast smoothie, all you need to do is place the ingredients from the list above into a blender and blend on high. You will want to do this for thirty seconds or until the smoothie has reached the desired consistency.
2. When it is done, pour into your favorite glass and top with extra blueberries and hemp seeds, if desired.

Nutrition Values:

Calories: 100

Protein: 12g

Fat: 70g

Carbs: 106g

Fibers: 23g

Chocolate Protein Smoothie

Time: Five

Servings: Two

Ingredients:

- Frozen Banana (1)
- Cacao Nibs (1 T.)
- Cocoa Powder (1 T.)
- Almond Butter (.25 C.)
- Almond Milk (2 C.)

Directions:

1. If you have a chocolate craving in the morning, this smoothie will be the perfect cure! Place all of the ingredients from the list above into your blender and blend on high until smooth. You can top this with extra cacao nibs for a little extra chocolate. Enjoy immediately!

Nutrition Values:

Calories: 380

Protein: 13g

Fat: 25g

Carbs: 30g

Fibers: 4g

Banana Protein Smoothie

Time: Five

Servings: One

Ingredients:

- Flax Meal (.50 t.)
- Vanilla Soy Milk (1 C.)
- Cannellini Beans (.50 C.)
- Frozen Banana (1)

Directions:

1. In the opinion of some people, this smoothie is so delicious—it almost tastes like a milkshake! To prepare this smoothie, place all of the ingredients from the list above into your blender and blend on high. You will want to make sure you use a frozen banana to make the smoothie cold. One smooth, pour into your favorite cup and enjoy!

Nutrition Values:

Calories: 340

Protein: 17g

Fat: 7g

Carbs: 60g

Fibers: 7g

Peanut Butter, Chocolate, and Coconut Smoothie

Time: Fifteen Minutes

Servings: Two

Ingredients:

- Almond Milk (2 C.)
- Raw Cacao Powder (2 T.)
- Maple Syrup (1 T.)
- Salt (.25 t.)
- Vanilla Powder (1)
- Peanut Butter (.33 C.)
- Frozen Bananas (3)

Directions:

1. For a smoothie that is a little sweeter, this may do the trick! If it is not sweet enough, you can always add a bit more maple syrup. To create this smoothie, simply place all of the ingredients from the list above into a blender and blend on high. By the end, you should have created a nice smooth consistency. All you have to do is pour and enjoy.

Nutrition Values:

Calories: 500

Protein: 20g

Fat: 25g

Carbs: 60g

Fibers: 8g

Vanilla Chai Smoothie

Time: Five Minutes

Servings: Four

Ingredients:

- Vanilla Extract (.25 t.)
- Chai Tea Bag (1)
- Vanilla Plant-based Protein (1 Scoop)
- Frozen Banana (1)
- Unsweetened and Vanilla Almond Milk (1.50 C.)

Directions:

1. To start off, you are going to want to heat your almond milk. You can do this on the stove or in the microwave. When it is hot, the almond milk will begin to steam. At this point, you will place your chai tea bag and steep it for five minutes or more. When this step is complete, place the tea into the fridge and allow to chill.

2. Next, you will want to remove the tea bag from the cup and add everything into your blender. Blend the ingredients on high until everything becomes nice and smooth. For an extra touch, try topping your smoothie with more banana slices and ground cinnamon!

Nutrition Values:

Calories: 100

Protein: 10g

Fat: 1g

Carbs: 20g

Fibers: 2g

"It's a Date" Smoothie

Time: Five

Servings: Two

Ingredients:

- Almond Milk (1 C.)
- Vanilla Extract (.50 t.)
- Dark Cocoa Powder (3 T.)
- Kale (1 C.)
- Pitted Medjool Dates (3)
- Frozen Bananas (2)

Directions:

1. If you are looking for something sweet, this smoothie offers a percent amount with delicious Medjool dates and cocoa powder. To create, all you have to do is place everything into your blender and blend on high until smooth. You can adjust any of the ingredients as needed. If the smoothie is too thick for your taste, just add more almond milk. When you have reached desired consistency, pour into a glass and enjoy.

Nutrition Values:

Calories: 170

Protein: 10g

Fat: 2g

Carbs: 42g

Fibers: 7g

Beet and Fig Smoothie

Time: Five Minutes

Servings: One

Ingredients:

- Unsweetened Almond Milk (75 C.)
- Nutmeg (.10 t.)
- Ground Cinnamon (.10 t.)
- Ice Cubes (5)
- Almond Butter (2 T.)
- Cooked Beet (.25 C.)
- Rolled Oats (.33 C.)
- Frozen Banana (1)
- Figs (3)

Directions:

1. Fig and Beet are both unusual to find in a smoothie but are actually quite delicious! When you are ready, place all of the ingredients from the list above into your blender and blend on high. While you can use raw beets, I suggest cooking them first so that it is easier to blend. For extra flavor, you can sprinkle your favorite granola on top. Enjoy!

Nutrition Values:

Calories: 640

Protein: 51g

Fat: 20g

Carbs: 75g

Fibers: 11g

Matcha and Kiwi Smoothie

Time: Five Minutes

Servings: Four

Ingredients:

- Ice Cubes (8)
- Water (2.50 C.)
- Salt (.10 t.)
- Raw Cashews (.33 C.)
- Avocado (.50)
- Kale (2 C.)
- Kiwi (2)
- Matcha Powder (2 t.)
- Stevia Powder (.10 t.)

Directions:

1. To create this delicious, green smoothie, simply place all of the ingredients from the list above into your blender and blend on high until smooth. If you would like your smoothie to be a bit sweeter, feel free to adjust the amount of stevia you use in it. You can also add more or less kiwi and kale depending on your taste. When you reach a smooth consistency, remove from the blender, pour, and enjoy!

Nutrition Values:

Calories: 150

Protein: 8g

Fat: 10g

Carbs: 15g

Fibers: 5g

Green Cleansing Smoothie

Time: Five Minutes

Servings: Four

Ingredients:

- Water (.50 C.)
- Almond Milk (.50 C.)
- Pineapple (1 C.)
- Chia Seeds (3 T.)
- Frozen Bananas (2)
- Super Greens (3 C.)
- Ice (as Needed)

Directions:

1. If you are looking to cleanse your insides, this smoothie will do the trick. All you have to do is add all of the ingredients from above into your blender and blend on high until smooth. You can use as little or as much ice as you would like to help create desired consistency. Enjoy immediately!

Nutrition Values:

Calories: 130

Protein: 6g

Fat: 4g

Carbs: 23g

Fibers: 4g

Conclusion

Congratulations! I hope that by this point in the book, you are convinced that as a vegan, you can consume the proper foods to achieve the nutrients that you need to thrive. There are going to be many doubters out there in the world—do not let them convince you that your diet is wrong. You are the only person you need to convince that a vegan diet is the best option for you.

You have made the decision to not only better your health but also make the world around you better. At this point, you are saving animals and helping the environment. Your diet choices are beneficial to you and the world around you. Now, you know just how delicious your diet can be. While some look at a vegan diet as restrictive, you know better. As a vegan, you get to have your cake and eat it as well!

As you become more comfortable with the recipes provided in this book, I invite you to add some ideas of your own! The best part of a vegan diet is how versatile it can be. If you have favorite vegetables, throw them in! There is no one way to cook—make it your own, and enjoy your diet every single day. I wish you the best of luck on your vegan journey. Now, let's get cooking!

Made in the USA
Middletown, DE
03 August 2019